PROSECUTING CHILD ABUSE:

AN EVALUATION OF THE GOVERNMENT'S SPEEDY PROGRESS POLICY

Joyce Plotnikoff

and

Richard Woolfson

BLACKSTONE
PRESS LIMITED

First published in Great Britain 1995 by Blackstone Press Limited,
9-15 Aldine Street, London W12 8AW.   Telephone 0181-740 1173

© J. Plotnikoff and R. Woolfson, 1995

ISBN: 1 85431 404 1

British Library Cataloguing in Publication Data
A CIP catalogue record for this book is available from the British Library.

Typeset by Style Photosetting Ltd, Mayfield, East Sussex
Printed by Bell and Bain Ltd, Glasgow

CONTENTS

Acknowledgements   ix

1 Introduction   1

Background — The scope of the study — Structure of the book — Postscript

2 The Government's Policy of Speedy Progress for Child Abuse Prosecutions   5

The commitment — The definition of 'child abuse' and cases to which the speedy progress policy applies — The lack of statistics — The need to evaluate the speedy progress policy for child abuse prosecutions

3 Methodology   11

Selection criteria for project cases — Identification of project cases by the CPS — Quality of data — Data collection — Interviews

4 Profile of Children and Study Cases   16

Case distribution — Children — Medical examinations — Defendants — Offences — Outcome of cases — Sentences

5 The Length of Time taken to Dispose of Study Cases   25

Time to disposition at magistrates' court — Time to disposition at Crown Court — Comparisons of Crown Court cases: defendant's plea and custody status — Recommendations of the Working Group on pre-trial issues

6 The Response of the Criminal Justice System:
The Police   32

Reporting the offence — Recording the crime — The investigation of offences
against children — The police decision to charge or summons an offender —
The designation of files as child abuse when referred by the police to the
Crown Prosecution Service — Informing the Crown Prosecution Service
about the child's ability to give evidence — The preparation of witness orders
and police procedures for 'warning' child witnesses

7 The Response of the Criminal Justice System:
The Crown Prosecution Service   43

Giving priority to child abuse cases — Identification of child abuse cases on
receipt from the police — Monitoring the progress of child abuse cases —
Consideration of notice of transfer to the Crown Court — Applications for
use of the TV link or screens on behalf of the child witness — Asking the
court for an expedited hearing, and making the prosecution's views known
on defence applications to adjourn child abuse cases — Return of brief by
prosecution counsel

8 Taking Account of the Child's Interests in the
Prosecution Process   52

The decision to prosecute: the role of police child protection units — The
decision to prosecute: the role of the Crown Prosecution Service — Child
welfare considerations in relation to other decisions — Communication
between the police and the CPS about the child's wishes and interests —
Therapy — Liaison with social services and the relationship with care
proceedings

9 The Response of the Criminal Justice System:
The Courts   65

The responsibility of courts to give priority to child abuse cases — Magis-
trates' courts — The identification of child abuse cases at the Crown Court
— The allocation of child abuse cases to the appropriate category of judge —
Crown Court policy and practice in listing child abuse cases — Crown Court
child liaison officers — Children's evidence at Crown Court: the use of live
TV links or screens — Videotaped interviews

10   The Management of Child Abuse Prosecutions   82

The characteristics of effective case management — The way forward

References   101

Index   105

ACKNOWLEDGEMENTS

This book was made possible through the support of the Trustees of the Nuffield Foundation who funded the research at a time when no government grant was forthcoming. The project was conducted under the auspices of the Institute of Judicial Administration of the University of Birmingham with the support of Professor John Baldwin, Institute Director, and Professor Ian Scott, Dean of the Faculty of Law.

The endorsement of the project by the Chief Crown Prosecutor for the Anglia Area, Robert Chronnell, greatly facilitated access to Crown Prosecution Service records and personnel. We received invaluable assistance from Roger Daw, Sharon Grace, Angela Palmer, Nicola Reasbeck, Alison Saunders and Julie Vennard of the Crown Prosecution Service Policy Group, Criminal Justice Policy Division. At the Lord Chancellor's Department, Beryl Branch, Mark Camley, Amanda Jeffery, Ann Nixon and Paul Zimmermann provided advice.

We are particularly indebted to Sarah Crayford-Brown of the Crown Prosecution Service and Julia Shales of the Lord Chancellor's Department who commented on the final draft and kept us up to date on relevant policy developments.

Data collection was based primarily in Crown Prosecution Service field offices, where we received the unfailing cooperation and courtesy of members of staff. Thanks are also due to the many others who contributed to the research, including police officers, staff of magistrates' courts, Crown Court centres, social services departments and Witness Service coordinators. Anonymity was promised to all fieldwork areas and interviewees, so we cannot acknowledge their contributions individually.

Lastly, we wish to acknowledge the 395 children whose cases form the basis of this study.

Alice looked round her in great surprise. '. . . Everything's just as it was!'

'Of course it is,' said the Queen. 'What would you have it?'

'Well, in *our* country,' said Alice, still panting a little, 'you'd generally get to somewhere else – if you ran very fast for a long time as we've been doing.'

'A slow sort of country!' said the Queen. 'Now, *here*, you see, it takes all the running *you* can do, to keep in the same place. If you want to get somewhere else you must run at least twice as fast as that!'

Through the Looking Glass by Lewis Carroll

ONE

INTRODUCTION

As a society, we find it difficult to acknowledge the suffering of children. The National Association for the Welfare of Children in Hospital reports that this is true even in the medical context ('Babies denied pain relief after surgery', *The Sunday Times*, 30 January, 1994). What safeguards can the criminal justice system provide to protect children from further distress when they are victims or witnesses of crime?

Although we lack precise statistics, it is acknowledged that prosecutions for assaults on children are increasing and more children are giving evidence at court. Despite the intention of recent reforms, too many child victims and witnesses continue to suffer at the hands of the system. A major worry is the delay in getting cases to court, despite an unequivocal commitment by the government to give child abuse cases priority. Are complaints about delays justified? If they are, why has the policy not worked?

Our criminal justice system is fragmented. At government level, responsibility for policy and administration is split between the Home Office (criminal policy, the police, probation and the appointment of magistrates), Lord Chancellor's Department (the Crown Court and magistrates' courts) and the Crown Prosecution Service (CPS). A further change occurred in April 1995 with the move to agency status for the Lord Chancellor's Department Court Service. The executive Court Service Agency is responsible for all Crown Court centres. Magistrates' courts (which are managed locally) remain the administrative responsibility of the Lord Chancellor's Department headquarters.

Locally, the police, courts and prosecutors have different structures and geographical boundaries. When a new criminal justice policy objective is introduced, clear directives are needed to ensure implementation across agencies. Without these, a 'duty gap' may develop because no one has responsibility for coordination and monitoring effectiveness. As a result, the criminal justice system fails to deliver the promised improvements. We believe that this has happened in the case of government policy to reduce delay in child abuse prosecutions.

Our book attempts to evaluate that policy and describe the response of each part of the criminal justice system to cases of child abuse. Because of the conveyor belt nature of the process, the professional participants – police, social workers, lawyers, prosecutors, court staff, magistrates and judges – tend to be familiar only with the stage in which they are personally involved. Different sets of lawyers and judicial officers deal with cases at magistrates' court and Crown Court. Police officers in child protection teams may attend court only when they themselves are witnesses, and neither they nor CPS lawyers (whose rights of audience are restricted to the magistrates' courts) routinely see children give evidence at Crown Court. Judges and barristers may have little insight into how cases are dealt with in the early stages of the investigation. We hope that the book will give an overview of how child abuse prosecutions are dealt with and prove helpful to those working to improve the treatment of children caught up in the criminal justice system.

BACKGROUND

The origins of this book go back to 1988, when Joyce Plotnikoff was working with the late Dr Jane Morgan on a Home Office study of child victims of crime (later published as Morgan and Zedner 1992) at the University of Oxford Centre for Criminological Research. On hearing the announcement of a new commitment by the government to give priority to child abuse prosecutions, the researchers were eager to identify the statistics prompting the concern and the means by which the new policy was to be measured. The discovery that neither yardstick existed led, eventually, to the funding of a two-year study by the Nuffield Foundation. The work was carried out between October 1991 and September 1993 by Joyce Plotnikoff, then research fellow at the Institute of Judicial Administration, University of Birmingham. Dr Richard Woolfson joined the project in 1992. The Department of Health and the Home Office funded an extension of this research for completion in August 1995.

THE SCOPE OF THE STUDY

The study was the first attempt to assess the effects of the 1988 government policy to expedite the prosecution of child abuse, and in particular, the provisions of the 1991 Criminal Justice Act, implemented in October 1992, which elevated the policy to a statutory level for the first time. The project was based on an examination of 200 prosecution case files and interviews with 85 criminal justice system personnel. It aimed to examine disposition times and to describe how the police, CPS and courts handled cases to which the government's policy of 'speedy progress' for child abuse prosecutions applies.

STRUCTURE OF THE BOOK

Chapter 2 describes the context of the government's policy commitment to expedite child abuse cases and some of the problems associated with it. A description of how the fieldwork was planned and carried out is contained in Chapter 3. A profile of the study cases, the children and defendants is provided in Chapter 4. Chapter 5 contains the key analysis of the length of pre- and post-Criminal Justice Act cases, comparing them with national statistics and the recommendations of the Working Group on Pre-Trial Issues.

The following four chapters address the response of criminal justice system agencies to child abuse prosecutions, and the extent to which they identify cases that come within the government's speedy progress policy. Chapters 6 and 7 describe the response of the police and CPS. Chapter 8 compares their responsibilities in taking account of the child's interests in the prosecution process. Chapter 9 examines the response of the courts.

Chapter 10 presents our findings and conclusions, including a discussion of factors contributing to delay, case management initiatives and good practice in the management of prosecutions involving child victims and witnesses.

POSTSCRIPT

In the autumn of 1994, partially as a response to this research, the CPS issued two new guidance documents for its staff. References have been added in the text and the main points are summarised here.

A new National Operational Practice Service Standard, 'According Priority to Child Abuse Cases', was issued to senior managers. This states that child abuse cases require sensitive handling by trained lawyers and caseworkers of appropriate experience to ensure that all relevant legal and policy issues are dealt with expeditiously. Consultation and liaison with other agencies involved in child abuse cases are emphasised. Preferential treatment is to be given to the delivery to counsel of the brief, which should note the importance of according priority to child abuse cases.

The National Operational Practice Service Standard introduces for the first time a requirement that CPS Areas maintain records of the time taken to deal with child abuse cases. (Reasons why we believe this is not a useful monitoring tool are discussed in our final chapter.)

Separate policy and casework guidance has also been issued about cases involving child witnesses. Previous guidance was scattered through various published and internal documents and its integration into a single document is a significant step forward. As an internal paper its status remains confidential, but it is being distributed to inter-agency committees and some agencies with whom the CPS has had particular contact in relation to child witness issues. Most of the points covered in the guidance involve clarification rather than a change in policy. Key points include the following:

The CPS has adopted the definition of child abuse set out in *Working Together under the Children Act 1989* (hereafter '*Working Together*') as the means of identifying cases to which the new Service Standard and best practice applies. For the purposes of CPS guidance, 'child' means a person under the age of 18 at the date of the offence. The guidance applies equally to victims and eye-witnesses. Some cases covered by CPS guidance do not trigger statutory procedures because the CPS definition covers a broader category than the Criminal Justice Act 1991. For example, the guidance covers children in the 14 to 17 age range who are not covered by the more restrictive statutory limits.

The best interests of the child should be the first – but not the final – consideration for the Crown Prosecutor when assessing the public interest.

Crown Prosecutors should ensure that cases involving child witnesses are expedited through the court process as far as possible and that they do not build any artificial hurdles when considering their evidence.

Crown Prosecutors should make use of all the procedures available to assist children when giving their evidence. In deciding whether to apply for use of the TV link or videotaped evidence, the best interests of the child should be considered. The effect on the jury of live evidence is not the primary consideration. Information should be obtained from the social services and/ or the police for inclusion in the application.

Crown Prosecutors should bear in mind the needs of child witnesses to be shielded, wherever possible, from unnecessary or unfair attack.

Crown Prosecutors cannot prevent therapy taking place but need to be aware that it may be thought to taint the evidence. They should request that they are informed if it is to take place and of its nature, and they should ask that the therapist notes its content.

Greater emphasis is placed on the use of notice of transfer provisions in s. 53 of the Criminal Justice Act 1991. Once a decision has been taken that a case should be heard in the Crown Court, eligible cases shall be transferred unless jurisdiction has been retained in the magistrates' court at the mode of trial decision, or the defendant faces a number of indictable offences only some of which qualify for notice of transfer.

In addition to the new Service Standard and guidance on child witness cases, the CPS has amended the Crown Court Case Preparation Package, a computer disk containing word-processed files, which provides standard language for inclusion in prosecution briefs to counsel. The amendments include options available for use in child abuse cases.

TWO

THE GOVERNMENT'S POLICY OF SPEEDY PROGRESS FOR CHILD ABUSE PROSECUTIONS

THE COMMITMENT

In discussing the impact of delay on children waiting to give evidence at court, the Lord Chancellor has acknowledged that 'Unnecessary stress cannot be in the interests of the unfortunate children involved and it certainly does nothing to further the interests of justice' (Spencer et al. 1990, p. 1). The recognition of these problems is not new. Over 30 years ago, the Magistrates' Association recommended a system of fast-tracking for cases involving assaults on children. At that time, delay was seen as a significant source of stress for children because after magistrates' court committal 'they may have to wait two or three months to give evidence . . . at the trial in a higher court' (Gibbens and Prince 1963, pp. 3, 20). Nowadays, when cases may take a year or more to reach trial, a wait of two or three months at the Crown Court is a laudable target.

Children experience the passage of time differently from adults. Delay in bringing child abuse prosecutions to court can have devastating consequences. It prolongs children's trauma and may also reduce their reliability as a witness. In our study, a despairing social worker wrote to the prosecution about a 14-year-old girl:

The time taken to deal with this matter has taken its toll on her. She interprets each further delay as a sign that no importance is placed on the offence . . . .. Obviously this will have dire consequences for her confidence as a witness. Both the girl and her mother have no trust left in the criminal justice system and feel they are being punished. I hope the prosecution barrister will have sight of this letter. My purpose is not to criticise but to highlight the problems which could jeopardise this case.

This trial collapsed after the girl gave evidence.

In 1988, Home Office Minister John Patten announced that guidance would be issued to ensure 'speedy progress' for child abuse cases. 'The damage done by child abusers to their victims must not be added to by avoidable delay in bringing criminal proceedings. These cases deserve high priority – they must be dealt with as quickly as possible' (Home Office news release, 'Child abuse cases to get greater priority', 18 February 1988).

The resulting Home Office Circular advised Chief Officers of Police to 'bear in mind the need to deal expeditiously with such cases in the interests of the child, and so help to minimise the time before the case comes to court' (52/1988, para. 25). The CPS issued similar advice. Official policy was restated in the 1990 Victim's Charter. 'The volume of business going through the courts means that priorities have to be set . . . An allegation of child cruelty or sexual abuse will always be given high priority' (Home Office 1990, p. 27).

In June 1988, the Home Secretary appointed Judge Thomas Pigot QC, the Common Serjeant of London, to chair an advisory group to consider the use of video recordings as a means of taking the evidence of children. The Home Office published the *Report of the Advisory Group on Video Evidence* in December 1989. Surprisingly, it failed to comment on the government's policy to expedite child abuse prosecutions but concluded 'It seems to us that one of the most substantial difficulties faced by children . . . is the extraordinary and, in our view, quite unacceptable delay which they must often endure before cases come to court' (para. 1.20).

The Pigot Report proposed a number of steps which, taken together, were intended to reduce pre-trial delay and stress for the child witness by capturing the child's testimony and cross-examination prior to the trial process:

> The best solution [to improve the position of the child witness at Crown Court] is one which is calculated to reduce delay, maximise the number of occasions on which flawed prosecutions do not proceed, and ensure that the preparation of cases which are to go to trial is accelerated. (para. 6.12)

Pigot recommended that a video-recorded interview with a child should be allowed in evidence and shown to the child in informal surroundings at a preliminary hearing outside the courtroom. The child could then be cross-examined, and the preliminary hearing would itself be videotaped and shown at trial. Committal proceedings at magistrates' court (at which the bench decides whether there is sufficient evidence to warrant jury trial at the Crown Court) would be circumvented.

Some of the Pigot recommendations were carried forward by provisions of the Criminal Justice Act 1991 which were implemented in October 1992. The admissibility of videotaped interviews was accepted, but only to replace evidence-in-chief, thus continuing to require the presence of the child in person for cross-examination at trial. The government rejected the central plank of the Pigot Report, that the child would not give live evidence at court unless he or she chose to do so. Addressing the problem of delay, s. 53 of the Act provided that in certain cases where a child will be called as a witness, the CPS has discretion to issue a notice of transfer bypassing committal proceedings and move a case directly to the Crown Court. For the first time, the Act placed a statutory duty on courts to 'have regard to the desirability of avoiding prejudice to the welfare of any relevant child witness that may be occasioned by unnecessary delay in bringing the case to trial' (Criminal Justice Act 1991, sch. 6, para. 7). The provisions apply not only to children who are victims but also to those who are eye-witnesses to sexual offences or offences of violence or cruelty. (Notice of transfer provisions are discussed in chapters 5 and 7.)

THE DEFINITION OF 'CHILD ABUSE' AND CASES TO WHICH THE SPEEDY PROGRESS POLICY APPLIES

There is no criminal offence of child abuse as such (Hall and Martin 1992, pp. 6–7; Wattam 1993, p. 2). With the exception of the notice of transfer provisions in the 1991 Act, the various versions of the general government policy to expedite child abuse prosecutions have failed to state what is meant by 'child abuse'. This is a blanket term covering a wide range of criminal offences as well as acts which may not be recorded as crimes by the police, such as emotional abuse or non-organic failure to thrive. The development of a separate civil child protection system focusing on the child's welfare, and use of the term 'abuse' rather than 'assault', may mean that the child is not even seen as a victim of a criminal offence (Morgan and Zedner 1992, pp. 86–87).

Child abuse is commonly understood to apply to activity occurring within families, but is also used in a wider context. The Criminal Injuries Compensation Board, which makes an increasing number of awards to child eye-witnesses and victims of violent crime, publishes 'examples of child abuse cases where the abuse occurred within and outwith the family' (*28th Annual Report 1992*). The government's speedy progress policy for child abuse prosecutions does not apparently exclude children who are victims of offences outside the family. Does it apply to cases involving children not expected to give evidence? What about child witnesses who are not themselves victims? Criminal justice system personnel to whom we spoke could not agree. The lack of a clearly understood definition for the group of cases to which the policy applies is likely to result in the inappropriate and unnecessary exclusion of some child victims or witnesses.

THE LACK OF STATISTICS

The speedy progress policy on child abuse cases provides a graphic demonstration of how gaps in government statistics limit the ability to monitor the effects of official policies (for example, Social Science Forum 1991; 'Statistics marred by blindspots', *The Times*, 26 September 1991).

Published statistics about the time cases take to reach disposition derive from information about defendants, not victims or witnesses. The right of all those accused of criminal offences to trial without undue delay dates back to the Magna Carta but was enshrined in statute only in 1985. Section 22 of the Prosecution of Offences Act 1985 empowers the Secretary of State to fix time limits on steps taken during the course of a prosecution and the length of time a defendant spends in custody prior to arraignment – the formal entry of a plea, which stops the clock on custody time limits. Regulations relate to indictable (i.e. the most serious) offences only and have imposed custody time limits which can be extended by the court for good cause. Victims and witnesses have no right to see the cases in which they are involved brought to a speedy trial and there has been no attempt to establish pre-trial time limits for child abuse prosecutions.

The focus of the criminal justice system is the defendant and statistics reflect this emphasis. There are no centrally collected national statistics about the total number of offences committed against children, except where the age of the victim is a component of the offence and a prosecution results. Offences such as unlawful sexual intercourse with a girl under 16 and indecency with a child are included, but rape and indecent assault are not. The Pigot Report stated:

> It appears to us to be highly desirable that more detailed national statistics about the victims of crime and the reasons for discontinuing or failing to proceed with potential prosecutions should be collected on an agreed basis and be made available to policy makers. In this context the questions which we wished to put – 'how many offences cannot be prosecuted because the principal witness or victim is a young child' and 'how often do prosecutions fail because child witnesses cannot cope with court procedures?' – simply could not be answered except in a limited, imprecise or anecdotal way. (para. 1.8)

No statistics are published about how long cases with child victims and witnesses take to get to trial. Even a special Home Office data collection exercise concerning offences against children did not address the question of time to disposition (Statistical Bulletin 42/89: Criminal Proceedings for

Offences involving Violence against Children). In 1991, the Lord Chancellor's Department asked Crown Court centres to provide information about time to disposition where a TV link application had been made. Although the results of the survey were not published, they were described to us as revealing 'endemic delay'. A 1991 Home Office study of cases involving 154 children giving evidence by TV link noted that the average time between the defendant being charged with the offence and the start of trial was 10.5 months (Davies and Noon 1991, p. 31).

There is little factual information about child witnesses in the legal system, even though as long ago as 1925 the Departmental Committee on Sexual Offences against Young Persons recommended that official statistics should record the number of offences against children. Spencer and Flin point out:

Despite official concern about the plight of child witnesses, no one in authority seems to have thought about keeping any kind of record of the number of children who are called as witnesses in legal proceedings, let alone in what capacity they are called, or in what type of case. (1993, p. 2)

More information about child witnesses is now being collected although it is not yet clear whether it will be published. The Lord Chancellor's Department has introduced two forms which are valuable sources of information. Since the introduction of TV links, Crown Court centres have been asked to complete the 'Children's Evidence Form' every time an application is made for evidence to be given via TV link and, since October 1992, for applications for video-recorded evidence to be presented in court. In January 1993, the 'Child Witness Form' was introduced for completion in all cases in which a child under 18 gives evidence in court. This provides information about applications for screens and children giving evidence in open court. Both forms include dates from which the time the case is pending at Crown Court can be calculated.

Initially, returns of these forms did not appear to include all possible cases. Enquiries during our fieldwork indicated that individual court clerks, who are usually responsible for their completion, sometimes forgot to do so or did not have a supply of forms. A particular weakness may be that the Children's Evidence Forms are likely to be overlooked in 'cracked' trials, where the child does not give evidence because the defendant pleads guilty at the last minute. The Lord Chancellor's Department has indicated that submission rates are improving.

THE NEED TO EVALUATE THE SPEEDY PROGRESS POLICY FOR CHILD ABUSE PROSECUTIONS

In rejecting the full package of Pigot Report recommendations, at least for the time being, the Lord Chancellor argued that time was needed to evaluate the reforms put forward in the 1991 Act: 'We shall then see whether they produce a really effective system for these trials to be conducted properly, quickly and at the right time' (Hansard 139-140, 21 May 1991). A few months later, Minister of State John Patten reiterated the need to wait to assess the impact of videotaped interviews and other reforms. He said the Lord Chancellor was giving attention to pre-trial delay and was considering how best to translate the statutory duty to avoid delay created by s. 53 into practical guidance:

> These reforms are pretty major changes in the law, and I think they will have an extraordinary impact after October 1992. . . . We shall be conducting research and close monitoring throughout to see how they are working. . . . (Hansard 1307-8, 28 February 1992)

A major project was initiated to evaluate the introduction of videotaped evidence, but no government funds were committed to research on delay in child abuse prosecutions or to evaluate the effectiveness of s. 53. The support for the research described in this book was provided by the Nuffield Foundation after an application for funding was rejected by the Home Office. The Department of Health and Home Office have now agreed to fund a 15-month follow-up study which started in 1994.

In the United States, where similar types of legislation have been introduced, 'laws giving priority scheduling to child abuse cases are rarely invoked. . . . These laws offer little more than a statement encouraging judicial and prosecutorial vigilance against unwarranted continuances' (Whitcomb 1986, p. 94). If the commitments in this country are to amount to more than 'encouraging statements', then evaluation and monitoring must be part of an on-going process.

THREE

METHODOLOGY

This chapter describes the selection criteria for project cases, how cases were identified by the CPS, the design of data collection instruments, the fieldwork and the range of interviews conducted.

SELECTION CRITERIA FOR PROJECT CASES

Our main aim was to look at the length of time taken to dispose of 200 child abuse cases in the light of government policy to give them priority. The work began with a three-month pilot study which examined the feasibility of various approaches to data collection. One option was to try to identify cases on receipt by a number of police forces and monitor their progress through the criminal justice system. However, at least some cases initially referred to the police are not made the subject of a crime report, and many do not proceed past the stage at which the police seek the advice of the CPS as to whether an alleged offender should be charged. (Pre-charge advice is not sought in all cases, and police referral rates to the CPS for such advice appear to vary according to locality. 'Criming' and 'advice' procedures are described in chapter 6.) The rates of attrition would probably have resulted in relatively few cases in such a sample reaching court.

The pilot study revealed that neither the police, nor the CPS nor the courts had adopted a consistent definition of child abuse. (In December 1991, the CPS issued guidance to field offices for the purpose of identifying cases to be expedited. This was updated in September 1994 – see chapter 7.) None of these agencies systematically identified cases involving child victims or witnesses, or collected information which would make it possible to monitor how long these cases took to disposition. On enquiry, it became evident that this was also true elsewhere in the country.

In the absence of consistent inter-agency practice, it was decided to base the data collection in CPS offices, where case files from a number of police divisions are concentrated. It was not feasible for us to screen all cases newly received by the CPS, because apart from the issue of the volume of cases involved, this would have required greater access to prosecution files than had been granted to the project. Agreement for access to CPS files was granted by headquarters on 15 December 1991 based on 'the very high public interest factor involved'. This agreement extended to specific files identified by CPS or requested by the researchers, but not to a 'trawl' through all files by the researchers in order to identify eligible cases. CPS headquarters undertook that local offices would try to identify child abuse cases for the study.

Cases identified in the first year of the study included 22 which terminated at magistrates' court, five juvenile court cases and six cases where the only child victim was aged under three. It was decided to narrow the range of enquiry by excluding these categories in the second year of the project. (A discussion of the ages of the children involved in project cases is included in chapter 4.) The prosecution of juveniles in youth courts is a separate process which would have required additional data collection resources. Nevertheless, this is a fruitful area for further study, because it is likely that a significant proportion of offences against children, including sexual offences, are committed by other juveniles (Glasgow et al. 1994). It was decided in the second year of the study to select only cases which had reached Crown Court.

For the main part of the fieldwork, cases were selected for inclusion in the project according to criteria established by s. 53 of the Criminal Justice Act 1991 which came into effect on 1 October 1992. Cases meeting the criteria are eligible to bypass committal proceedings. This process, which was first applied to serious fraud cases, gives the Director of Public Prosecutions the discretion to issue a notice of transfer moving a case directly to the Crown Court for the purpose of avoiding any prejudice to the welfare of the child. (Transfer procedures are described in chapter 7.) CPS staff were therefore asked to identify cases committed for trial, or which were eligible for notice of transfer and which involved a potential child witness:

(a)   where the child was under 14 (or under 15 if the child was under 14 when a videotape was made of the interview with the child) if the offence involved violence or cruelty; or

(b)   where the child was under 17 (or under 18 if the child was under 17 when a videotape was made of the interview with the child) if the offence was sexual.

Section 53 applies not only to child victims within the family, but also to those who are the victims of stranger assaults, and to eye-witnesses of sexual offences or offences of violence or cruelty. This provided a further reason for adopting the s. 53 definition for project cases. Interviews indicated that children who were eye-witnesses but not victims, or who were the victims of assaults outside the family, often fell outside participants' perception of cases to which the speedy progress policy should apply. The project provided an opportunity to look at the application of new procedures to this wider category of children. The timing of the project allowed us to monitor 100 cases before s. 53 was implemented and a further 100 cases in its first year of operation.

It should be noted that the choice of cases falling within the s. 53 criteria meant excluding those in which the child was considered too young to be a potential witness. Cases of cruelty, neglect, and assaults on babies which clearly constitute child abuse did not come within our terms of reference.

IDENTIFICATION OF PROJECT CASES BY THE CPS

In the first year of the project, 100 pre-Criminal Justice Act cases were drawn in equal numbers from the pilot district and three other CPS areas in different parts of the country. The sample incorporated closed and pending cases which had begun as much as 12 months prior to the fieldwork.

Although all approached the task with great good will, these four CPS offices responded in different ways to the request to identify project cases in accordance with s. 53 criteria:

(a) A Principal Crown Prosecutor responsible for one CPS magistrates' court section instituted a log at the beginning of the project. The CPS Crown Court section identified pending and closed cases, and in the second year of the project also instituted a log.

(b) A Branch Crown Prosecutor identified a mix of pending and closed magistrates' court cases. The CPS Crown Court section identified some pending cases then instituted a log for incoming cases. In this area the CPS task was facilitated because some, though not all, relevant cases were flagged by the police as 'Victim's Charter', i.e. sensitive cases requiring special treatment (for further detail, see chapter 6).

(c) A Branch Crown Prosecutor identified magistrates' court and Crown Court closed and pending cases.

(d) Closed and pending cases were identified by the CPS Crown Court section, mostly from a chronological log of all cases received which listed offences. A clerk checked those which seemed most likely to have juvenile victims.

In the second year the sample was drawn from post-Criminal Justice Act cases which entered the magistrates' court system shortly before or after implementation of s. 53 in October 1992 and which were eligible for notice of transfer. It quickly became apparent that three of the four original fieldwork areas were unlikely to yield their quota of post-Act cases. Two additional CPS offices (one from a new area) were asked to identify cases meeting the criteria, and as a result a further 31 cases were added in order to make up the 100 cases in the post-Act sample.

Visits were made to each location in which cases were identified and files were monitored until completion. At the end of fieldwork during the summer of 1993, 24 Crown Court cases had not reached plea or trial, and in others the defendant had not yet been sentenced. In 1994 we attempted to complete the data collection effort during follow-up visits to the fieldwork areas. We were unable to obtain information about all outstanding cases because of the difficulty in tracing closed files. The study therefore includes 14 cases for which the outcome at Crown Court was not available, and a further six cases in which the defendant's sentence is unknown.

QUALITY OF DATA

No conclusions can be drawn about the representativeness of the study sample because none of the methods of case identification was particularly systematic. In studies such as this, it is always a matter of concern that the existence of the research itself will affect case selection or the performance of observed cases. While these possibilities cannot be ruled out, there is no indication that any effect was significant. If study cases were the subject of special attention, then processing times are even longer than the research suggests.

DATA COLLECTION

A data collection instrument for use with CPS files was developed which covered the progress of all cases from magistrates' court through Crown Court and recorded details under a range of headings, including the offence, victim/witness, police interview, involvement of social services, the alleged offender, court activity and case outcome.

CPS files are a fruitful source of information for a project of this type, but they have limitations. For example, they do not record all the stages which court staff go through in scheduling the case for hearing. Referral to different types of court records is necessary for such a task, and this was beyond the scope of this project except in a few cases. Thus it was not possible to identify the first date on which listing action was taken by the Crown Court to schedule a case for hearing, a factor which appears to be significant in the overall time to disposition of Crown Court cases (Plotnikoff and Woolfson 1993, p. 36). Nor was it possible to rely on CPS files to provide information about the manner in which a child gave evidence. CPS caseworkers attending court may cover several courtrooms, and may not always be able to note what takes place at trial. In some cases, police officers were contacted to provide supplementary information about whether children gave evidence in open court, by TV link or with screens.

In the second year of the study, the data collection instrument was amended to reflect issues raised by the 1992 *Memorandum of Good Practice on Video-recorded Interviews with Child Witnesses for Criminal Proceedings*. We noted whether a videotaped interview was used in court proceedings. The project also examined reports to the CPS for information required by the *Memorandum* 'about the wishes of the child, and his or her parents or carers, about going to court' and whether the CPS file reflected a need to seek further information from the joint investigation team on this question (para. 2.14).

INTERVIEWS

During the pilot stage, interview schedules were developed. These addressed definitions of child abuse, responsibility for the speedy progress policy, the processing of cases involving child victims and witnesses, information flows between criminal justice system participants, and perceptions of delay.

Over the two years of the study, discussions were held with 85 criminal justice system personnel, involving the CPS (senior staff, lawyers and caseworkers), police (senior managers and officers in child protection and administrative units), magistrates' courts, Crown Court centres (clerks, listing officers and child liaison officers), social services (senior managers in child protection and social workers) and coordinators of court-based Witness Service units. As required by the terms of our access, interviews with CPS personnel did not address decision-making in specific cases.

In the second year of the project, interviews were conducted with three newly designated Crown Court child liaison officers who were appointed in centres with TV link facilities. They have responsibility for a range of functions relating to child witnesses, including monitoring the progress of the case through liaison with the listing office (May 1992, guidance issued by the Lord Chancellor's Department).

A conference between CPS, police and counsel was observed in one case and the scope of such meetings was discussed with CPS personnel and the police. Crown Court listing procedures and meetings with barristers' clerks were observed, as were committal proceedings and the testimony of child witnesses in a small number of cases.

It was beyond the scope of this project to interview children or their carers (for a study of the impact of crime on children, see Morgan and Zedner 1992). Where CPS files noted the impact of the offence or the prosecution process on the child, this was recorded.

FOUR

PROFILE OF CHILDREN AND STUDY CASES

This chapter provides details of the children, defendants, offences, case outcomes and sentences in project cases.

Totals for pre- and post-Criminal Justice Act cases are provided separately only where useful for purposes of comparison. Some categories of information were not available in all prosecution files. For this reason, totals in some of the tables below account for fewer than the 200 cases in the study sample.

CASE DISTRIBUTION

The project examined 200 cases from a wide distribution of sources. Cases were dealt with by six police forces, five CPS Areas, 44 magistrates' courts and 17 Crown Court centres.

CHILDREN

A total of 395 children were victims or witnesses in the 200 cases in the study sample. More than half (106 cases) involved only one child, but 74 involved two or three children. The largest number involved in a single case was 13.

Number of children involved per case

Children	1	2	3	4	5	6	7	11	13
Cases	106	51	23	7	3	5	3	1	1

Detailed information was recorded for a maximum of four children per individual case. They accounted for 362 of the 395 children involved in study cases. The following tables provide information about these 362 children. A substantial minority were boys.

Gender of child		Kind of witness	
Male	Female	Victim	Bystander
115	247	317	45

A small proportion of these 362 children (45 = 12·5 per cent) were not victims of crime but bystander witnesses. Davies and Noon's study of child witnesses in England and Wales identified 11 per cent who were bystanders (1991, p. 23), in contrast with Scottish research by Flin et al. which found that 51 per cent of children called as witnesses were bystanders (1993). In the absence of a more comprehensive survey of child witnesses in English courts, the difference between the jurisdictions is probably explained by the Scottish rule of evidence which requires every criminal offence to be proved by the evidence of at least two witnesses (Spencer and Flin 1993, p. 2).

Ages of children

1	2	3	4	5	6	7	8	9	10	11	12	13	14	15	16
3	3	7	9	12	16	19	28	33	36	39	48	29	47	21	12

The children's ages ranged from one to 16. The average age of both boys and girls was between 10 and 11. The issue of children's ages as a basis for selection for the case sample is discussed in chapter 3.

Section 52 of the Criminal Justice Act 1991 was intended to abolish the competence requirement for child witnesses. (For a discussion as to whether s. 52 actually abolished the competency requirement, see Spencer and Flin 1993, p. 64. The Criminal Justice and Public Order Act 1994 clarifies the issue, allowing the child's evidence to be excluded only on the basis that the child is incapable of giving intelligible testimony.) Section 52 came into effect on 1 October 1992 and inserted a new section, s. 33A, into the Criminal Justice Act 1988. This provided that all children under 14 shall give evidence unsworn in criminal proceedings, ensuring that there is no lower age limit for child witnesses and that 'the court will not be required to undertake a special examination of a child because of his age before he is allowed to give evidence in criminal proceedings' (Home Office Circular 6, 1992).

It was expected that this change in the law, combined with the admissibility of videotaped interviews, would result in cases being prosecuted which involved younger children: '. . . it seems, following the enactment of s. 52, that one cannot draw a fixed minimum age at two or three years since it depends on the nature of the evidence to be given and the ability of the particular child to communicate' (Wasik and Taylor 1991, p. 125). Prior to October 1992 when the changes became effective, comments in CPS files from police or prosecutors concerning very young children generally opposed their giving evidence. For example, counsel's advice regarding a three-year-old was that 'she is too young even to give unsworn evidence, and I envisage some difficulties in the event of trial'. Charges involving an assault on a four-year-old were dropped before committal, even though she had given a consistent account. The file recorded the comment of the prosecutor that, 'a four-year-old cannot be regarded as a viable witness'. However, the police officer in a case with a five-year-old described him as 'bright, alert and of above average intelligence' and suggested that he give evidence, with screens, at a magistrates' court old-style committal as well as at Crown Court.

After October 1992, there was no apparent change in the number of younger children coming to court or in the approach of lawyers. For example, after a conference with counsel in a post-Act case it was decided not to proceed with a count involving a five-year-old. The lack of impact of the Act's provisions may be due in part to the fact that a significant proportion of all cases involving children of seven and under also involved older children who may have been considered more capable of giving evidence. Seven children aged seven or under actually gave evidence at Crown Court in pre-Act cases (three aged seven, two aged six, and two aged five) but only two in this age range testified in post-Act cases. Five of these trials resulted in convictions and four in acquittals. Of the remaining 33 cases involving at least one child aged between three and seven, 24 resulted in guilty pleas, three in convictions and three in acquittals. Two were dismissed without trial and one had not finished by the end of the study.

MEDICAL EXAMINATIONS

At least one child was medically examined in 98 of the 200 cases. The roles of the doctors conducting the examinations were as shown in the table below.

Role of doctor conducting medical examination of child

Police surgeon	Paediatrician	Joint exam	General Practitioner	Role unknown
32	28	17	14	7

Seventy-seven of the cases in which a medical examination took place had reached completion by the end of fieldwork. Out of 22 cases in which no medical evidence was found, 13 resulted in conviction and six in acquittal (three others were discontinued at magistrates' court). In 47 cases where medical evidence could be described as 'consistent' with the alleged offences, 37 resulted in conviction and 10 in acquittal. In 16 cases in which medical evidence could be described as 'supportive' of the allegations, 12 resulted in convictions and four in acquittals.

DEFENDANTS

Gender of defendant		Age of defendant			Kind of court	
Male	Female	under 17	17–20	21 and over	Adult	Juv
189	11	9	16	175	195	5

Number of co-defendants					Other cases outstanding?	
0	1	2	4	5	Yes	No
186	9	3	1	1	27	173

Was defendant in custody for any part of pre-trial period?		Type of bail for defendants on bail throughout pre-trial period	
Yes	No	Conditional	Unconditional
43	157	135	22

Of the 200 cases, 186 concerned defendants acting alone. In the 14 cases with co-defendants, information was recorded about the first-named defendant only.

Most defendants were male, over 21 and remanded on conditional bail. (Further information about conditional bail is provided in chapter 6.) They were most commonly known to the child (neighbour, babysitter or friend of the family, a relative or member of the same household).

Relationship of defendant to first child

Known adult	75
Father	25
Relative other than those listed	27
Stepfather	16
Mother	11
Parent's cohabitee	16
Stranger	15
Known juvenile	6
Teacher	4
Sibling	5
Stepmother	0

OFFENCES

Offences are divided by seriousness into four classes for allocation to the appropriate level of judge (see chapter 9). Attempted murder is a class 1 offence, rape is class 2, and buggery is class 3. The most common offence in the study cases, indecent assault, is an example of a class 4 offence.

Class of offence

1	2	3	4
3	38	14	145

Three out of four defendants were charged with more than one count; one defendant was charged with 37 counts.

Number of counts

1	2	3	More
50	30	70	70

The following table relates to the principal charge in each of the 200 study cases.

Nature of offence

Indecent assault	97
Rape	26
Buggery	13
Gross indecency with child	12
Actual bodily harm	9
Cruelty/neglect	8
Indecency with child	7
Incest with girl of 13 or over	6
USI with girl under 13	6
GBH/wounding s. 18	4
GBH s. 20	3
Attempted murder	3
USI with girl of 13 or over	3
Robbery	1
Taking indecent photos/video of children	1

OUTCOME OF CASES

Outcome of magistrates' court cases

	Pre-Act	Post-Act
Plead guilty	10	0
Convicted after trial	6	0
Dismissed without trial	6	1
Acquitted after trial	1	0
TOTAL	23	1

Outcome of Crown Court cases

	Pre–Act	Post–Act
Convictions	51	63
Acquittals	23	20
Indictment to lie on file	3	2
Unfinished cases at end of fieldwork	0	14
TOTAL	77	99

Five study cases ended with the indictment lying on file. In two of these the defendant did not enter a final plea, in another two the defendant pleaded guilty and no jury was sworn, and in the last case the defendant pleaded not guilty and a jury was sworn.

Crown Court convictions

	Pre–Act	Post–Act
Plead guilty to partial/amended indictment	17	25
Plead guilty to full original indictment	13	28
Jury verdict	21	10
TOTAL	51	63

Crown Court acquittals

	Pre–Act	Post–Act
Judge ordered	7	4
Judge directed	6	4
Jury verdict	10	12
TOTAL	23	20

Broadly, a directed acquittal occurs after the trial has begun, often as a result of a submission by the defence but sometimes at the judge's own instigation. It is distinguished from a judge ordered acquittal which occurs before the trial begins, usually because the prosecution are unable or unwilling to offer any evidence.

In total, 83 out of the 157 cases finishing at Crown Court in conviction or acquittal were guilty pleas. This plea rate of 53 per cent compares with a national figure (Judicial Statistics 1992, para. 12, p. 57) of 69 per cent of guilty pleas among all cases committed for trial in 1992. In fact, national figures count a case as a guilty plea only if all defendants plead guilty, while our study cases selected only the first defendant. Cases which result in the indictment being left to lie on file are excluded both from the national plea rate and the study figure. The low plea rate appears to be related to the higher than average proportion of acquittals in study cases. Forty-three (27 per cent) of the Crown Court study cases resulted in acquittals, while national figures (Judicial Statistics 1992, para. 13, p. 57) show that 16 per cent of all defendants dealt with at Crown Court during 1992 were acquitted. (The comparison is valid as only a single defendant was selected in study cases involving multiple defendants.) The difference is not due to the prosecution case being more likely to collapse: 28 per cent of study cases where a not guilty plea was entered were dismissed on the order or direction of the judge, compared with a national figure of 37 per cent. (This figure can be deduced from tables 6.7 and 6.9 on p. 61 of Judicial Statistics 1992). Nor were juries less likely to convict in study cases: 49 per cent of jury trials resulted in convictions compared with a national figure of 45 per cent (tables 6.9 and 6.10, pp. 61 and 62 of Judicial Statistics 1992). The higher incidence of acquittals in study cases is therefore likely to be related to the smaller proportion of defendants who entered a plea of guilty.

SENTENCES

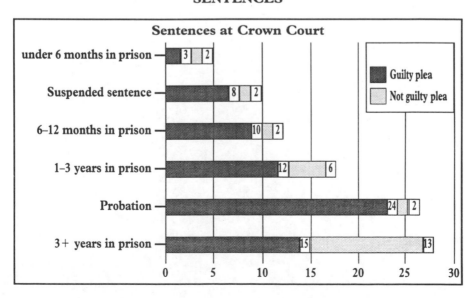

There were eight cases with disposals not represented in the table on p. 23: five ended in community service orders, one with a fine, one in a s. 37 hospital order and one with a conditional discharge.

In post-Act cases it was noted whether the sentence included a condition of treatment. Only five sentences included such a condition. Provision of treatment schemes in prison and the probation service is uneven. Home Office policy requires that sex offenders imprisoned for four years or more should be assessed immediately after sentence to determine which are most in need of treatment, but it seems that resources are not available to guarantee treatment for all offenders even in this category (Sampson 1994, pp. 106, 111).

FIVE

THE LENGTH OF TIME TAKEN TO DISPOSE OF STUDY CASES

Our case sample consisted of 100 cases dealt with at magistrates' court or committed for trial before October 1992, and 100 cases in which committal or notice of transfer proceedings were held after October 1992 when the child witness provisions of the Criminal Justice Act 1991 were implemented. All of the 100 pre-Act cases and 86 of the post-Act cases had reached plea or trial by the time the study finished.

This chapter compares pre- and post-Act cases with separate national statistics for disposition at magistrates' court and Crown Court. Both pre- and post-Act cases routinely took longer to reach disposition than the national average. Completed post-Act cases moved somewhat more quickly than pre-Act, but this may not be true for the average post-Act case as 14 were still unfinished at the close of fieldwork.

Notice of transfer procedures, introduced specifically to reduce delay in child abuse prosecutions, were seldom used in our post-Act cases. The 11 notice of transfer cases moved more quickly through the magistrates' courts, but the eight which had completed by the end of fieldwork actually took longer on average to dispose of at Crown Court than other study cases.

Of study cases which were completed, 23 took more than a year from first magistrates' court appearance to disposition at the Crown Court, the longest taking over 23 months. A further 19 cases took over nine months. The average for cases tried at the Crown Court was over 10 months. However, it is not possible to compare overall duration of study cases with national figures. The Home Office and Lord Chancellor's Department collect separate statistics for magistrates' courts and Crown Court centres and these cannot be combined to reflect the duration of cases from first appearance in magistrates' court to the start of trial, plea or other disposal in the Crown Court.

The chapter also compares the performance of study cases with time intervals recommended by the Working Group on Pre-Trial Issues. Most Crown Court trials in the study sample exceeded the recommended period from committal to trial in bail and in custody cases.

TIME TO DISPOSITION AT MAGISTRATES' COURT

The table below shows the number of days taken to dispose of study cases in the magistrates' court, and includes cases which terminated there as well as cases which proceeded to the Crown Court, via committal proceedings or notice of transfer. National figures referred to in the table relate to indictable offences (all study cases were in this category) and are drawn from Home Office Statistical Bulletin, 19 November 1992. Figures relate to June 1992 and are taken from tables 1 and 2.

Waiting times in days at magistrates' court

	National figures	Study cases before CJA (number of cases)	Study cases after CJA (number of cases)	
			No notice of transfer	Notice of transfer
first to last appearance	63	82 (98)	73 (88)	–
first appearance to notice of transfer	not available	not applicable	–	54 (11)

Study cases took longer than the national average of 63 days from first to last appearance at magistrates' court. Pre-Act cases took an average of 82 days. Post-Act cases moved somewhat more quickly with an average of 73 days from first to last appearance (calculated for the cases in which committal proceedings were held).

TIME TO DISPOSITION AT CROWN COURT

In the second year of the study, new procedures were introduced by the Criminal Justice Act 1991 allowing magistrates' court committal proceedings to be bypassed by notice of transfer. These provisions apply in certain categories of child witness cases, and were intended to reduce delay by giving the CPS the discretion to move a case immediately to the Crown Court (the process is explained in more detail in chapter 8).

National figures in the table below are taken from Lord Chancellor's Department Judicial Statistics: Annual Report 1991, table 6.14, p. 63 (covering the calendar year). In 1992, the national average for the time from committal to start of final hearing was 96 days, i.e. longer than the previous year, but nevertheless faster than the average time to disposition for post-Act cases. The time from committal to the start of the final hearing is defined as:

The actual time between the committal (or date of execution of the bench warrant) and the start of the hearing. The start of the hearing is defined as the date of the arraignment, if the defendant is dealt with then, or the date on which the jury is sworn, if this occurs on a later date. (letter to the authors from the Lord Chancellor's Department, 10 December 1992)

Waiting times in days at Crown Court

	National figures	Study cases before CJA (number of cases)	Study cases after CJA (number of cases)	
			No notice of transfer	Notice of transfer
committal to start of final hearing	88	182 (77)	125 (77)	–
notice of transfer to start of final hearing	not available	not applicable	–	144 (8)

The 77 pre-Act Crown Court cases took, on average, 182 days from committal to the start of the final hearing, over twice as long as the national average of 88 days. Post-Act, 77 completed cases committed for trial finished on average in 125 days. However, it cannot be concluded that post-Act cases reached plea or trial more quickly, because 14 cases were still unfinished at the close of fieldwork.

Notice of transfer was used in two of the five fieldwork areas in a total of 11 project cases. The previous table shows that use of notice of transfer resulted in a average saving of 19 days at magistrates' court (54 days compared to 73 days for other study cases). However, our eight completed notice of transfer cases actually took an average of almost 20 days longer to dispose of at Crown Court than study cases which had been committed for trial (144 days compared to 125 days). Schedule 6 of the Criminal Justice Act 1991 allows the defendant to apply for dismissal of a transferred case at the

Crown Court which is a potential cause of delay, but this procedure was not invoked in any of the project cases.

COMPARISONS OF CROWN COURT CASES: DEFENDANT'S PLEA AND CUSTODY STATUS

The following table compares pre- and post-Act cases with national statistics for the time from committal or notice of transfer to start of the final hearing according to the defendant's plea and custody status. For comparison purposes, the study sample was divided according to the defendant's final plea. Cases scheduled as trials but where a guilty plea was entered on the day of trial are counted as guilty pleas. National figures are drawn from Judicial Statistics 1992, table 6.17, p. 64.

Days from committal/notice of transfer to start of final hearing

	Custody	Bail	Guilty plea	Not guilty plea
Pre-Act study cases	200	177	111	226
Post-Act study cases	120	130	109	155
National figures	78	102	80	123

The table illustrates that pre- and post-Act cases were disposed of more slowly than the national average across all four categories. As noted above, it would be premature to conclude that post-Act cases as a whole reached plea or trial more quickly, because 14 post-Act cases were still unfinished at the close of fieldwork.

RECOMMENDATIONS OF THE WORKING GROUP ON PRE-TRIAL ISSUES

The report of the Working Group on Pre-Trial Issues was published in 1990. The Group was chaired by the Lord Chancellor's Department and consisted of representatives of the CPS, Home Office, Justices' Clerks' Society, the Legal Secretariat to the Law Officers and the police. The Law Society and Bar were not represented. The report set out to establish best practice and common standards throughout the criminal justice system. The report emphasised the need for national guidelines at each stage of Crown Court proceedings. The report has been accepted in full by Ministers, and its recommendations have been taken forward in a National Implementation Plan with individual agency initiatives.

The CPS is required to 'accord priority status to cases of child abuse' (Standing Commission on Efficiency 1990, para. 21.5; National Operational Practice Service Standard, 'According Priority to Child Abuse Cases', 1994). In practice, this is interpreted as conducting cases, to the extent possible, within the time intervals recommended by the Working Group (advice to the researchers from the CPS Inspectorate). The following tables contrast time intervals for pre-trial stages recommended by the Working Group ('PTI recommendations') with the time taken by study cases.

Magistrates' court: either way offences tried summarily at the magistrates' court (bail cases)

Either way offences are those which are triable on indictment at the Crown Court or summarily at the magistrates' court. Indecent assault, the most common offence in the study sample, is triable either way. The decision as to which court should try these cases is taken at mode of trial proceedings in the magistrates' court. In our study, all defendants accused of either way offences who received summary trial were on bail. All of the summary trial cases were in the pre-Act sample.

Either way offences tried summarily (bail cases)

	First appearance to mode of trial	Mode of trial to summary trial (not guilty pleas only)
Study cases	26	77
PTI recommendation	28 (recommendation 69)	56 (recommendation 77)
Number of study cases exceeding PTI recommendation	7 out of 19	6 out of 10

Where the defendant is to be tried summarily, a plea is usually taken for the first time at the mode of trial hearing. Recommendation 77 allows a maximum of 56 days between the entry of a not guilty plea and summary trial. Where a full file of evidence is available from the police at the plea hearing and the defence have prepared their case, the recommended interval drops to 28 days (recommendation 78).

Magistrates' court: first appearance to committal proceedings or notice of transfer (indictable only offences)

A number of serious crimes are purely indictable offences which must always be tried on indictment in the Crown Court.

First appearance to committal/notice of transfer in indictable only offences

	Custody	Bail
Pre-Act study cases	76	88
Post-Act study cases	71	53
PTI recommendation	42 (recommendation 81)	56 (recommendation 83)
Number of study cases exceeding PTI recommendation	26 out of 30	13 out of 27

Magistrates' court: first appearance to mode of trial, and mode of trial to committal or notice of transfer (either way offences)

Either way offences committed or transferred for trial

	First appearance to mode of trial		Mode of trial to committal	
	Custody	Bail	Custody	Bail
Pre-Act study cases	26	24	46	62
Post-Act study cases	7	19	39	62
PTI recommendation	14 (recommendation 68)	28 (recommendation 69)	42 (recommendation 81)	56 (recommendation 83)
Number of study cases exceeding PTI recommendation	3 out of 13	19 out of 97	5 out of 13	40 out of 97

Crown Court: committal or notice of transfer to trial

The Working Group on Pre-Trial Issues made recommendations relating to Crown Court waiting times between committal and trial where a not guilty plea was entered. Study cases where a trial was held have been chosen for the purpose of comparison.

Committal or notice of transfer to trial

	Custody	Bail
Pre-Act study cases	292	202
Post-Act study cases	167	163
PTI recommendations (recs. 115–116)	56	112
Number of study cases exceeding PTI recommendations	13 out of 13	45 out of 53

The comparisons with national figures for case processing times in this chapter demonstrate that cases in the study sample were, by almost all measures, slower than the national average. They also exceeded many of the time intervals recommended by the Working Group on Pre-Trial Issues. The following chapters describe how cases were dealt with by the criminal justice system and explore some possible reasons for delays.

SIX

THE RESPONSE OF THE CRIMINAL JUSTICE SYSTEM: THE POLICE

This chapter describes the reporting of the offence to the police and procedures surrounding recording the crime, the investigation stage, the decision to charge or summons a suspect and the identification of 'child abuse' files when forwarding papers to the CPS.

In our project, specially trained officers in police child protection units (CPUs) investigated most alleged offences committed against children within the family or by someone *in loco parentis*, such as a teacher or babysitter. However, such officers did not deal with all young victims and witnesses. Stranger assaults were more likely to be dealt with by uniformed officers or the Divisional CID. Only children dealt with by CPUs were interviewed on videotape or in the presence of a social worker. CPU involvement increased the likelihood that comments concerning the child's ability as a witness would be communicated to the CPS and that applications for the use of a TV link would be made. Proportionately, the CPS was twice as likely to apply for use of the TV link on behalf of children dealt with by police officers in CPUs than for those interviewed by CID or uniformed officers. Also, information about the child's wishes and interests was more likely to be supplied to the CPS by CPUs (see chapter 8).

The criminal justice system response was therefore determined more by the nature of the offence and whether there was a relationship with the offender than by the age and needs of the child.

REPORTING THE OFFENCE

Reports of offences against children usually reach the police in a roundabout way. Partial revelations by children, particularly of sexual offences, are not unusual and reporting may be delayed for a considerable period of time. Project cases came to light in a wide range of ways, including disclosures prompted by the discovery of pornographic photographs, the arrest of an adult male client with a 'rent-boy' and in response to the broadcast of a TV programme about child abuse, as well as through reports to teachers, parents, schoolfriends and social workers.

Time between offence and reporting to the police

	Number of cases
Under a week	122
A week to a month	8
1–6 months	27
6–12 months	7
1–2 years	7
Over two years	14

Information was available in 185 of our 200 cases about the time which elapsed between the offence and when it was reported to the police. We recorded the date on which an offence was alleged to have taken place or the latest date of offences alleged to have taken place over a period of time, but did not distinguish these categories. (Only 50 of the 200 cases involved a single count offence and many of the other cases involved offences over time.) Although most offences were reported within a week, in 28 cases reporting was delayed for more than six months, and half of these offences were reported over two years later. The date of the report to the police and the circumstances in which the offence was revealed were not always clearly stated in the police case summary provided to the CPS, and were sometimes not even apparent from an examination of witness statements. Prosecutors described this category of information as an important part of their assessment of the case, particularly as the circumstances in which offences are revealed can be used by the defence to discredit children.

RECORDING THE CRIME

Policy requires that the police record an alleged offence on a numbered crime form immediately after it is reported, a process described as 'criming'. These forms are also used to record the outcomes of cases and form the basis of most crime statistics. All the cases in this study had been crimed.

Not all reports of child abuse are crimed (Morgan and Zedner 1992, p. 87). Sometimes the failure to enter an alleged offence on a crime report relates to perceptions about the offence, for example cases of child neglect investigated by the police rarely seem to reach a crime report. Officers acknowledged that some offences against children are not recorded on a crime report because they would have to be classified as unsolved (police child protection units tend to have very high clear-up rates on intra-familial offences, either because there is an admission or because the identity of the offender is known). Others fail to be crimed even though they could be classified as 'cleared up' in official police statistics (for example, a matter dealt with under civil child protection proceedings). It was not possible to explore the effect of such practices in this study, but clearly crime reports do not reflect all reported offences against children.

THE INVESTIGATION OF OFFENCES AGAINST CHILDREN

Nature of police response in study cases

Category of case	Dealt with by by CPU	Dealt with by routine police procedures	Not known whether dealt with by CPU
All cases	156	27	17
Social worker present at interview	97	0	4
Defendant relative or household member	90	2	8
Defendant known to children but not in family or household	64	15	6
Defendant unknown to children	2	10	3

Police child protection units

Following the publication of the *Report of the Inquiry into Child Abuse in Cleveland 1987*, most police forces established specialist child protection units, known by a variety of names but referred to here as CPUs. These units are increasingly likely to be part of the CID structure (the detective branch as distinct from uniformed officers), interviewing offenders as well as children, and the officer in charge of the case (the 'OIC') may be part of the

CPU. Children in 156 of the 200 study cases were interviewed by officers in CPUs.

Although initially set up to deal with sexual abuse within the family, many CPUs now have a broader remit. For example, the terms of reference of several fieldwork CPUs covered any situation 'where the child does not receive the proper standard of care a reasonable parent can be expected to give. The term [child abuse] embraces sexual and physical abuse, emotional neglect, non-organic failure to thrive and non-accidental injury'.

Typically, CPUs conduct investigations 'within the family and extended family', including any person entrusted with the care of the child at the time of the alleged offence (for example school staff or youth workers) and regular visitors to the household such as neighbours and family friends. Most of the study cases dealt with by CPUs consisted of sexual offences alleged to have been committed by relatives or members of this wider group.

Children dealt with by conventional police methods

Specialist officers do not deal with every child victim or witness encountered by the police. The terms of reference for CPU work did not extend to responsibility for child victims of stranger attacks. Only two out of 15 such cases in the study sample were known to have been assigned to CPUs. Officers in different areas commented that the time of day at which such an offence is reported may influence the type of police response. CPU officers are usually not on active duty during the night. Our sample contained one case in which the child victim was described as a 'rent-boy'. Beverley Hughes of the School of Social Work, University of Manchester, drew our attention to the fact that although child prostitution may be a manifestation of organised abuse, such cases seem more likely to be dealt with by the Vice Squad and CID without reference to the child protection system. There may be little awareness of what these cases involve in terms of how such boys are recruited and the physical and psychological damage they often experience.

Government advice states that the conduct of videotaped interviews should be restricted to specialist police and social work teams with 'appropriate training and regularly employed in joint childcare investigations' (*Memorandum of Good Practice 1992*, p. 2). Thus children initially dealt with by uniformed or CID officers need to be referred to CPUs if a videotaped interview is to be made. None of the study cases dealt with by conventional police methods had interviews which were videotaped. (Videotaped interviews are discussed further in chapter 9.)

One police force in a fieldwork area acknowledged the need to be able to videotape interviews with children in cases not handled by CPUs. It intended to respond to this problem by training a number of non-CPU officers to conduct video interviews with child victims of non-family offences. These officers will not receive full CPU training, and it remains to be seen whether they will receive sufficient referrals to develop an adequate level of expertise.

CPUs attributed their inability to deal with all child victims and witnesses to rising workloads and limited resources. However, they also identified other constraints. They were not confident that they would always be notified about child victims and witnesses who came to the attention of fellow officers. A special obstacle is what one CPU sergeant described as the 'traditional grip' of the CID on witness interviews. A chief inspector in another area commented that the CID may not recognise the expertise available in the CPUs, and spoke of the need for further general police training on the evidential benefits of child interviews conducted by specially trained personnel.

Joint interviews with the child by police and social workers

Increasing emphasis has been placed in the past five years on the joint investigation of child abuse by police and social workers (Home Office Circular 52/1988; *Working Together* 1988, revised edition 1991; *Memorandum of Good Practice* 1992). Social workers were present when children were interviewed in 97 out of 200 study cases, all of which were dealt with by CPUs; there were no examples of social workers attending an interview with a child conducted by CID or uniformed officers.

Seeking pre-charge advice from the Crown Prosecution Service

Where time permits, the police may seek the advice of the CPS in deciding whether to proceed to charge. If the CPS does not accept the case at this 'advice stage', it is dropped. Information as to how many child sexual abuse cases were referred to the CPS and were not proceeded with is not centrally recorded (Hansard 411, 29 June 1993). Both police and CPS acknowledged that pre-charge consultation may be used not only where there is a genuine question of law or evidence but also, in the eyes of families or social workers, to shift the responsibility to the CPS for not proceeding with cases seen as 'no-hopers'. Although all study cases proceeded into the court system, it was not possible to discover to what extent pre-charge advice had been sought. Requests and responses are supposed to be recorded in writing, but in practice this can be an informal process and advice given by telephone was not always documented.

One CPS area kept a log of child abuse cases indicating whether they were received as a charge, summons or advice case. Over a 12-month period, 27 per cent were advice cases and it was estimated that four out of five resulted in no further action. Another CPS area estimated that at least 50 per cent of advice cases are declined. Prosecutors said that in advice cases, they relied heavily on police assessments of the child witness (see below).

THE POLICE DECISION TO CHARGE OR SUMMONS
AN OFFENDER

In the table below, national figures relate to June 1992 and are taken from tables 1 and 2 of the Home Office Statistical Bulletin, 19 November 1992.

Time intervals prior to committal/ transfer

	Average no. of days from offence to charge/summons	Average no. of days from charge/summons to first appearance	Average no. of days from offence to final magistrates' court appearance/ notice of transfer
Pre-Act cases	173	11	266
Post-Act cases (committals)	176	13	263
Pre-Act cases (notice of transfer)	51	13	118
National figures	43	23	129

The table illustrates that study cases took four times as long as the national average of 43 days from the offence to the formal start of the prosecution process, when the offender is charged or summonsed to appear in court. Study cases took approximately twice as long as the national average from the offence to final appearance or notice of transfer in the magistrates' court. These delays are almost entirely due to the delays in reporting to the police described above, and not to the investigation of the offence. For pre-Act cases, the average time from reporting to charge was 26 days (based on available information for 88 cases), in comparison with 36 days for post-Act cases (based on information for 98 cases). However, CPUs reported that occasionally the decision to charge may be delayed to enable the views of a child protection case conference to be taken into consideration.

The table identifies one of the few time intervals where project cases moved more quickly than the national average, namely from charge or summons to first appearance in the magistrates' court. There are two reasons for this. The study sample contained 43 cases in which the defendant was in custody for some or all of the time between first court appearance and the end of the case. Where the defendant is in police custody, cases must be brought to court soon after the defendant is charged. The other reason is the high proportion of study cases in which conditions were imposed on the defendant's bail (135 of 157 study bail cases). The police cannot impose conditions on the defendant if they release him on 'police bail' and therefore bring to court quickly those cases in which they wish conditions to be imposed. Some of the conditional bail cases were also produced from custody. The police and prosecution asked for a custodial remand but the magistrates released the defendant on conditional bail. Conditions (typically requiring the defendant not to contact the child witness, or to stay at a specified address) must be imposed by the magistrates' court. Under the Criminal Justice and Public Order Act 1994, police are given the power to grant conditional bail.

The table also indicates that in study cases, notice of transfer was issued by prosecutors in cases which were reported to the police relatively promptly.

THE DESIGNATION OF FILES AS CHILD ABUSE WHEN REFERRED BY THE POLICE TO THE CROWN PROSECUTION SERVICE

In the first year of our study, none of the police forces we visited routinely marked or flagged cases as 'child abuse' (for example, by writing this on the file or cover document) when forwarding papers to the CPS. In the second year, one area's CPUs started flagging child abuse and domestic violence cases for the attention of the CPS.

Elsewhere, a police force and CPS area responded to the 1990 Home Office *Victim's Charter* with a joint initiative requiring the police to attach a coloured card to certain files referred to the CPS. The card states, 'this file has been "tagged" in respect of the Victim's Charter. Should the circumstances of the defendant change (i.e. release from custody etc.) please inform the [police] administrative support unit immediately'. The tag scheme was introduced in January 1991, and allows a detective inspector to give '*Victim's Charter*' status to a range of cases, including those with a young or vulnerable victim or witness. The accompanying advice states that the attachment of the coloured tag 'is intended to convey that the file requires special consideration by all who come into contact with it'. However, the guidance focuses on improved communication with the victim about the progress of the case or changes in the defendant's bail or custody status, and does not urge that such cases be given priority. Nineteen of the 41 study cases in this area had been tagged by the police. A few child abuse cases which were tagged had not been entered on the CPS Crown Court section child abuse log.

In the second year of the study, in response to the call of the Working Group on Pre-Trial Issues for greater standardisation, a front sheet (Form MG1) was introduced nationally for the transmission of files from the police to the CPS. This form incorporates a box for 'special category cases', which the accompanying instructions describe as cases which 'must be highlighted in order to afford them priority. For example, child abuse . . .. The decision whether a file is a special category case is a policy decision and not a personal one'. Sixty CPS case files contained the standard front sheet, but only 25 of them were marked 'special category'.

INFORMING THE CROWN PROSECUTION SERVICE ABOUT THE CHILD'S ABILITY TO GIVE EVIDENCE

Under the Criminal Justice Act 1991, children are assumed to be competent witnesses, though a case may still not proceed because an individual child is not considered competent to give evidence (*Memorandum of Good Practice* 1992, para. 2.13 and margin note). The only evidence in the case may be the word of the child. The prosecutor takes into consideration the impression witnesses are likely to make and how they are likely to stand up to cross-examination. Because prosecutors do not interview witnesses themselves, in seeking to make an informed decision about calling a child witness the prosecutor may watch a videotaped interview, if one exists. Otherwise, the prosecution are reliant on the police to provide relevant information.

Of the 100 pre-Act cases, 25 contained an assessment of the child's ability as a witness in the police records transmitted to the CPS. In 1992, the police introduced a new standard Confidential Information Form MG6. Guidance for its use was amended in 1993 and officers are required to identify to the CPS any witness or victim in a 'vulnerable' category, expressly including children, and to notify the CPS of their special needs. The MG6 requests information in relation to several categories, including 'comments on the strength and weakness or vulnerability of the witness'. However, only 52 post-Act cases contained an assessment of a child's ability to give evidence.

Assessments of the children were provided in almost half of the cases in which children were interviewed by CPU officers, compared with one-third of the remainder. However, even in these cases there was a great deal of local variation. A minority of CPUs had produced almost all of the assessments identified.

The *Memorandum of Good Practice* encourages interviewing teams to consider the child's chronological age and then, 'assess the apparent developmental stage the child has reached, taking an overview of cognitive, linguistic, emotional, social, sexual, physical and other development, and the child's attention span' as well as the child's concept of time, cultural background and any disabilities (paras. 2.3–2.10). Very little information of this depth is reflected in reports to prosecutors.

Assessments often stated little more than whether the child would make a good witness. Positive comments included:

> 'The children are mature for their age and would give good credible evidence.'
> 'She gave evidence at committal and is an intelligent witness. She gave a good impression albeit a little overconfident.'
> 'He found it quite difficult to talk about what happened but would be able to relay it.'
> 'The child has a speech impediment and lisp and speaks quietly, but should make a good witness.'
> 'The child [attending a special school] is very simple and not capable of making up the disclosure.'

Assessments very occasionally referred to obtaining information about the child from other sources, for example:

> 'These children have been assessed by a psychiatrist and their cognitive development is below average.'
> 'Her teacher says she is honest, of average intelligence, and does not normally lie or exaggerate.'

Sometimes comments amounted to suggestions that the child should not give evidence, or would have a great deal of difficulty:

> 'L is a disturbed child. His behaviour since the allegations came to light has been extremely erratic. He is not a good witness.'
> 'This child would be a poor witness – too traumatised.'
> 'Y is very distraught and upset – she could only describe the act of intercourse after writing it down.'

THE PREPARATION OF WITNESS ORDERS AND POLICE PROCEDURES FOR 'WARNING' CHILD WITNESSES

Witnesses at magistrates' court committal proceedings, even those whose evidence is in the form of written statements, must be made the subject of an absolute or conditional order to attend the Crown Court trial (Criminal Procedure (Attendance of Witnesses) Act 1965, s. 1). The defence is supposed to notify the prosecution as to whether it requires prosecution witnesses to give evidence at trial, in which case such witnesses are 'absolutely' or fully bound. Witnesses not so identified are 'conditionally' bound. Witness orders must be served 'as soon as practicable' after the defendant has been committed for trial (Magistrates' Courts Rules 1981, r. 8(1)).

The preparation of witness orders at magistrates' court committal proceedings has been described as 'one of the major causes of difficulty' by the Working Group on Pre-Trial Issues. The Working Group reported complaints from Crown Court staff, the CPS and the police that witness orders made at committal were often ill-considered and did not accurately identify the witnesses eventually required to give evidence at court (paras 221, 222). The Group recommended that it would be more appropriate for witness orders to be made at the Crown Court once the required number of witnesses had been established (para. 223).

The difficulties identified by the Working Group on Pre-Trial Issues were borne out in study cases, where it was not uncommon for there to be uncertainty about whether the child was required as a witness until the last minute. Comments in some files reflected that no TV link application had been made for this reason. The defence often issued 'blanket' witness requirements, that is witnesses were either all fully or all conditionally bound. Defence solicitors reportedly tell committal proceedings that final witness requirements cannot be decided until counsel is briefed, which usually does not occur until after committal. In one of the project areas, it was part of the local legal culture for the defence routinely to request only conditional witness orders at magistrates' court committal proceedings, requiring the police to do extra work in checking witness availability and making it very difficult for the prosecution and the Crown Court to plan effective listings for trial.

Blanket witness requirements obviously contribute to uncertainty for the child witness, but other problems were also identified. Witness 'warning' is the process by which witnesses are told about the probable trial date (procedures by which cases are listed for trial are described in chapter 9). For each prospective trial, the CPS completes a 'List of Witnesses to Attend Court' (the 'LWAC' form), used to inform the police about which witnesses are required. (The form has colour-coded carbon copies, and is also used to record the payment for court attendance.)

Police administrative support units usually warn witnesses, but CPU officers often prefer to do it themselves because of the sensitivity required. (One of the provisions of 'tagged' cases described above was that witness orders were to be handled by the original officers.) However, the officers responsible for the case were not always notified about witness orders even where they had previously requested them. Errors occurred because, as one inspector said, 'it is an exception to the loop of routine police procedures'. CPU officers cited examples of children becoming very distressed when 'warned' by conventional administrative support unit methods (letter, phone call or visit from a police officer not previously involved with the case). An example noted in CPS files involved a 12-year-old girl in a children's home who received the witness warning by mail. 'It worried her so much that she went onto the roof and it took staff a long time to get her down.'

Some police officers expressed concern about how witness warning would be carried out in sensitive cases if the CPS took over responsibility for this function. The *Guide to Pre-Trial Issues within the Crown Prosecution Service* discusses this possibility but recommends that in the case of vulnerable witnesses, the responsibility should remain with a police officer in the case (p. 27).

In order to enable CPU or other officers who interview children to warn their own witnesses, it is necessary to identify appropriate cases as they progress through the system. Cases in the project sample, as we have seen, were not routinely flagged. In addition, child witnesses were not routinely identified as juveniles on LWAC forms. In the pre-Act case sample, 111 children were absolutely bound witnesses but only 26 were identified as juveniles on these witness lists. Post-Act, 143 children in 75 cases were absolutely bound. In only 47 of these cases were the children identified on the lists as juveniles. Only one case in the study sample contained instructions in the CPS file to 'make it clear on the witness list that these children are juveniles'.

SEVEN

THE RESPONSE OF THE CRIMINAL JUSTICE SYSTEM: THE CROWN PROSECUTION SERVICE

This chapter describes the responsibilities of the CPS which include:

(a) giving child abuse cases priority;

(b) the identification of such cases on receipt from the police;

(c) monitoring their progress;

(d) consideration of whether notice of transfer provisions should be used to move eligible cases directly to the Crown Court;

(e) consideration of applications for use of TV links or screens;

(f) asking the court for an expedited hearing; and

(g) making the prosecution's view known on defence applications to adjourn child abuse cases.

CPS guidance to its staff is not published. Much of the policy information to which we refer was provided by the CPS Policy Group and the now disbanded National Field Inspectorate. At the time our research was conducted, policy requirements discussed in this and the following chapter were not gathered together in a single document for the guidance of prosecutors. In September 1994, the CPS issued collective guidance to staff about cases involving child witnesses. It states that 'The CPS fully supports the notion that children are a class of victims and witnesses to whom special care should be paid. Delay should be avoided in all cases involving a child victim or witness'. The accompanying National Operational Practice Service Standard, 'According Priority to Child Abuse Cases', directs prosecutors to ensure that such cases are expedited through the court process as far as possible. The guidance and the Service Standard are summarised in the Introduction to this book.

GIVING PRIORITY TO CHILD ABUSE CASES

The CPS is required to give priority status to child abuse cases (lStanding Commission on Efficiency 1990, para. 21.5; National Operational Practice Service Standard 1994, 'According Priority to Child Abuse Cases'). In practice, this is interpreted as conducting cases, to the extent possible, within the time intervals recommended by the Working Group on Pre-Trial Issues. However, as discussed in chapter 5, these were often exceeded by study cases.

IDENTIFICATION OF CHILD ABUSE CASES ON RECEIPT FROM THE POLICE

Independently o the policy requiring the police to identify child abuse cases forwarded to the prosecution, CPS policy requires that child abuse files be identified on receipt.

In December 1991, the CPS issued its staff with a working definition of child abuse for the purpose of implementing the government's speedy progress policy, the only criminal justice system agency to do so. It described its first priority as expediting cases in which the child is a victim: 'If all cases came within the definition of "child abuse" it would defeat the object . . . as the increase in cases . . . would cause the systems to overload.' The CPS definition excluded eye-witnesses (although these are covered by notice of transfer provisions) and child witnesses to other issues of fact (to whom videotape interviews and TV link provisions extend) 'because these cases are very difficult to identify at first glance. If it is discovered, at the review stage, steps can then be taken to ensure that the case is expedited' (letters from CPS Policy Group, 20 October and 23 December 1992).

In September 1994, after our research was completed, the CPS issued superseding guidance, adopting the definition of child abuse set out by the Home Office, Department of Health, Department of Education and the Welsh Office in *Working Together*. This defines child abuse by reference to the presence of neglect, physical injury, and sexual or emotional abuse. The 1994 CPS guidance applies to a broader category of children, including eye-witnesses.

Despite the fact that CPS had issued its own definition of child abuse in 1991, only one of the CPS fieldwork areas made a systematic attempt to identify these cases on receipt (see chapter 3). Out of the 200 study cases, only 51 CPS files were marked, flagged or logged as child abuse, and local practice showed much variation. Sometimes files were marked 'child abuse' on the CPS magistrates' court file folder but not on the CPS Crown Court file folder, or vice versa. A new, pre-printed CPS file folder has been introduced, but it does not have a box for this type of identification.

The CPS office mentioned above logged cases on receipt at magistrates' court level. In the second year of the study two CPS Crown Court sections introduced lists to record receipt of child abuse cases. (They should be distinguished from security logs which the CPS is required to keep of cases with videotaped interviews.) Even where such lists had been introduced, some study cases identified through other sources had not been included. There did not appear to be any difference between cases logged and those which were not.

MONITORING THE PROGRESS OF CHILD ABUSE CASES

The existing CPS computer system collects management information for the calculation of performance indicators, including projections of average processing delay. It is not used to track the progress of child abuse cases. It is not clear whether the new CPS standard case management and tracking system (SCOPE) will have this facility.

The CPS is required to keep the progress of child abuse cases under constant review to prevent avoidable delay (Standing Commission on Efficiency 1990, para. 21.5; National Operational Practice Service Standard 1994). CPS guidance requires child abuse cases to be passed on receipt to a senior prosecutor for monitoring to ensure they progress in timely fashion. While individual CPS staff acknowledged the need to give priority to child abuse cases, the research did not identify any procedures for providing management information to senior legal staff by which the effectiveness of the speedy progress policy could be measured. The CPS Policy Group pointed out that our findings somewhat contradict a 1991 survey carried out 'which found excellent monitoring procedures in force' in a number of CPS areas (letter, 11 April 1994).

When our fieldwork was conducted, CPS case preparation for magistrates' court and Crown Court hearings was organisationally separate. Magistrates' court cases were dealt with by teams of lawyers. Crown Court work was undertaken separately by teams of caseworkers (law clerks) who briefed counsel, among other responsibilities. The involvement of CPS lawyers in magistrates' court sections more or less ceased when cases passed to the CPS Crown Court section, usually in a different physical location. Neither section monitored information relating to the length of proceedings. The CPS is now undergoing internal reorganisation as a result of which lawyers and caseworkers will work in teams, with the goal of promoting greater continuity of processing throughout the duration of the case.

Of the three CPS logs mentioned in the previous section, only one recorded dates relating to the progress of the case and could have been used to calculate the time to disposition at Crown Court, though not the duration of the case as a whole because it did not record the date of first appearance at the magistrates' court. However, this log was not always up to date.

Senior lawyers also have responsibility for review of case files (including decisions about notice of transfer, see the following section) and their allocation to lawyers of appropriate experience. The project attempted to collect information about the date of the first file review but recording of this information varied according to local practice.

Although the National Operational Practice Service Standard states that child abuse cases require 'sensitive handling by experienced and trained lawyers and caseworkers', this does not mean that they are always prosecuted by specialists. The CPS takes the view that prosecutors should be able to handle a broad category of work. In the past it has avoided the identification of specialists, with the exception of the prosecution of young offenders. The prosecution of child abuse is one of many subjects in which staff lawyers receive in-service training. Some CPS areas (including three of our fieldwork offices) have designated lawyers with a degree of special responsibility for child abuse cases. This is considered a matter for local management. These lawyers did not handle all child abuse cases but were available to consult with colleagues and the police, and often contributed to inter-agency training. Their role did not extend to formal monitoring of the progress of child abuse cases. For example, one Principal Crown Prosecutor reported that she tried to keep an eye on Crown Court lists and asked the CPS Crown Court section to let her know what happened but acknowledged this did not constitute monitoring. Some caseworkers responsible for Crown Court work had developed particular sensitivity to the needs of child witnesses, though none had received special training. Even where such a caseworker was responsible for preparing the case, he or she did not necessarily attend court when it was dealt with.

CONSIDERATION OF NOTICE OF TRANSFER TO THE CROWN COURT

For a detailed account of these procedures, see the Act itself (and also, for example, Wasik and Taylor 1991, pp. 126–8). The Criminal Justice and Public Order Act 1994 amends the requirements for notice of transfer.

Eligibility

The Criminal Justice Act 1991 extended to some cases involving child witnesses a procedure first introduced in 1987 in complex fraud cases. Section 53 gives the Director of Public Prosecutions discretion to issue a notice of transfer, moving certain child witness cases directly to the Crown Court. The procedure can only be used for the purpose of avoiding any prejudice to the welfare of the child. Notice of transfer to bypass magistrates' court committal proceedings may be issued:

(a)   if the evidence is sufficient for the person charged to be committed for trial; and

(b) if the child was a victim or eye-witness of the offence and is either –

(i)   under 14 and the offence involves violence or cruelty; or
(ii) under 17 and the offence was sexual.

The age limits are increased by one year if the child was under the appropriate age when a videotaped interview was made. The relevant date for determining age under the Act is the date on which notice is served.

Section 53 applies not only to child victims within the family, but also to eye-witnesses to sexual offences or offences of violence or cruelty, and to victims of stranger assaults. It is, however, more restrictive than eligibility for use of the TV link which includes children who are not eye-witnesses but simply witnesses to a fact in issue at the trial. Selection of study cases was based on s. 53 eligibility. We therefore had to exclude the case of a child, called to give evidence placing the defendant at the scene of a murder, but who was not an eye-witness to the crime. Spencer and Flin (1993) comment that the s. 53 restriction to eye-witnesses is unnecessarily restrictive: 'Not for the first time, fussy and over-detailed drafting ends up leaving tiresome holes' (p. 87).

The right to appeal

Grounds of appeal for dismissal of the notice of transfer are limited. The certification that transfer is in the interests of child cannot be challenged. Procedures allow for the defendant to apply for dismissal of the case at a pre-trial hearing in the Crown Court but the child cannot be called. None of the transferred study cases was the subject of an appeal application.

Timing of the decision to issue notice

Guidance to prosecutors states that they should make the decision to issue a notice of transfer at the earliest opportunity. In either way offences, by law, notice must be served before examining magistrates begin committal proceedings. However, the CPS guidance states that prosecutors should issue notice at an earlier stage, prior to the mode of trial decision. (At a mode of trial hearing in the magistrates' court, the decision is made in either way cases as to whether they should be dealt with at magistrates' court or at the Crown Court.) If the prosecutor chooses not to transfer the case because a summary trial is considered appropriate but the defendant elects Crown Court trial or the magistrates decline jurisdiction, prosecutors are advised to issue notice in order to remove the case directly to the Crown Court and avoid committal proceedings.

Monitoring notice of transfer cases

No guidance has been issued to CPS staff about logging the occasions on which notices are issued, or monitoring the length of time transferred cases take to disposition. Because child abuse cases themselves were not identified with consistency, CPS staff were unsure how many cases might be eligible for notice procedures. New guidance issued in 1994 places greater emphasis on CPS use of notice of transfer procedures, but does not require them to be monitored.

Experience of notice of transfer provisions

Although all of the 100 post-Criminal Justice Act study cases were eligible for notice of transfer, the procedures were used in only two of the five post-Act fieldwork areas in a total of 11 cases. Prosecutors gave a number of different reasons for their reluctance to use notice of transfer provisions:

(a)   It is a mistake to consider notice provisions hurriedly, therefore it is difficult to issue them, as required, before a mode of trial decision.

(b)   Risk versus speed (notice should not be used to transfer weak cases, because it is a higher risk strategy to bypass committal).

(c)   Statements of evidence to be served with the notice may be vulnerable to defence review.

(d)   There is confusion as to whether charges can be added or the indictment amended (a relatively common practice) after transfer.

(e)   Notice of transfer does not necessarily result in a faster trial. (Those who had used it felt that they had gained only a week or so benefit, borne out by the research findings (see chapter 5).)

(f)   These cases are more time-consuming to prepare (though others suggested that preparation for committal and transfer is very similar).

(g)   A decision cannot be made until the full file has been received from the police.

(h)   Notice should be used only if the defence are delaying matters or ask for an old-style committal.

(i)   The removal of the defence's right to require the presence of a child witness at an old-style committal is a far more significant protection, and makes the use of notice of transfer unnecessary in most cases.

Many prosecutors concluded that the number of occasions on which it was appropriate to use the procedures was relatively limited, and this view was borne out by the experience of study cases. In five of the six project cases for which information was available, the mode of trial decision occurred before the case was transferred. The CPS had not considered these cases suitable for summary trial. This suggests that the decision to transfer the case was reactive, made in response to the defendant electing Crown Court trial.

Prosecutors also seemed more willing to issue notice where the defendant had made admissions; four notice cases ended with the defendant pleading guilty. New CPS guidance issued in 1994 states that for either way offences, if the prosecutor decides that Crown Court trial is appropriate, the notice should be served promptly and, in any event, before the mode of trial decision.

APPLICATIONS FOR USE OF THE TV LINK OR SCREENS ON BEHALF OF THE CHILD WITNESS

In cases to which s. 32 of the Criminal Justice Act 1988 applies, the CPS should consider whether evidence should be given by a child witness through a television link (Standing Commission on Efficiency 1990, para. 14.1; see Introduction, above). In appropriate cases, application on Form 5308 should be made to an officer of the Crown Court within 28 days of the date of committal proceedings at the magistrates' court. (Extensions are routinely granted. In practice, applications for TV links are made by the CPS, though they can be made by the defence.) Apart from the question of advance notice to the Crown Court so that the trial can be scheduled for a courtroom equipped for TV link use, it is in the interests of the child to be told as early as possible how his or her evidence is to be given. Over the two-year study, 29 out of 60 applications for the TV link were made out of time, on average 76 days after committal. (Information was available for 55 out of 60 cases in which an application was made.) Delays in making applications often seemed to be due to uncertainty as to the defendant's plea and whether the child would be required to give evidence. For example, in one case the defendant had made admissions in his statement and a guilty plea was anticipated, but he entered a not guilty plea at a pre-trial hearing.

In a small number of cases, late consideration of the need for TV links required a transfer between courts (from a court with no facilities to one with the equipment) and was a significant cause of delay. CPS records reflected little consideration of this question by lawyers prior to committal.

There is no time requirement for applications for the use of screens at Crown Court trials. In study cases, such applications were made an average of 88 days after committal. (Information was available for 35 out of 39 cases in which an application was made.)

ASKING THE COURT FOR AN EXPEDITED HEARING, AND MAKING THE PROSECUTION'S VIEWS KNOWN ON DEFENCE APPLICATIONS TO ADJOURN CHILD ABUSE CASES

CPS lawyers should endorse the file if they ask the court for an expedited hearing. Only five CPS files included a written request to the Crown Court asking for a priority listing. The CPS places emphasis on asking the court for fixtures in child abuse cases, that is a fixed date for trial. Unfortunately, a fixture usually precludes a priority listing, something acknowledged in one of our cases where the CPS caseworker asked the listing officer not to fix the case because it would result in excessive pre-trial delay. (Problems relating to Crown Court listing are discussed in greater detail in chapter 9.)

When a defence application is made for the adjournment of a child abuse case, the CPS is required to 'ensure that the court is made aware of public concern about the effects of delay upon child victims and witnesses' (Standing Commission on Efficiency 1990, para. 21.5). CPS files did not reflect whether objections were made in court to defence-generated requests for adjournments. Only one case included instructions in the brief to counsel to 'resist delay'. The 1994 National Operational Practice Service Standard, 'According Priority to Child Abuse Cases', requires counsel to be notified in instructions of the importance of according priority to child abuse cases.

RETURN OF BRIEF BY PROSECUTION COUNSEL

The CPS itself does not present the prosecution case in the Crown Court. Instead, it is represented by a barrister retained on a case-by-case basis (barristers are independent and often do both prosecution and defence work). The CPS prepares a written brief to the barrister of its choice with details of the evidence and other information. The term 'return of brief' is used to describe the situation when the first counsel engaged by the CPS or defence solicitor is unable to appear at court. Philip Ely, former President of the Law Society, described the frequency with which briefs are returned as a 'running sore which reflects badly on the whole profession' (Reeves 1991, p. 70). The timing has a critical effect on preparation for court as many briefs are returned on the eve of a hearing. The head of the government legal service and the Director of Public Prosecutions have reported that over half of all prosecution briefs to counsel are returned within 48 hours of Crown Court hearings (joint submission to the Lord Chancellor's Advisory Committee on Legal Education and Conduct, 18 October 1992). Although hearings fixed to a specific date accommodate the prior commitments of all barristers involved, briefs may be returned even in these cases, sometimes because earlier trials run over or for other, less valid reasons.

In 25 out of 40 pre-Act Crown Court trials, the first-briefed prosecution counsel did not appear. First-briefed counsel did not appear in 15 out of 27 post-Act trials. (The problem is believed to occur less frequently with defence briefs.) A barrister may be reluctant to read the brief properly and advise if he is unlikely to appear at trial. Late consultations take place because of last minute changes of counsel, and new barristers sometimes take a different view of the case (Plotnikoff and Woolfson 1993, pp. 44–7). This may result in a late change of plan about use of the TV link (see below).

Although the phenomenon of returned briefs is a particular problem for the prosecution, only two project case files noted any attempt to tackle this directly. In one, a Principal Crown Prosecutor advised the CPS Crown Court section, 'choice of counsel will need to be made very carefully in this case and it should be made plain to counsel who is instructed that it will not be acceptable for the brief to be returned at a late stage'. In the other case, the prosecution brief stated:

> In the event that a prior or unexpected commitment will make it impossible for counsel to present this prosecution personally, he is asked to ensure that his clerk notifies the instructing solicitor [CPS] forthwith so that there may be adequate time to discuss the passing of papers to alternative counsel, and if this course is acceptable to instructing solicitors for it to be approved.

The matter of return of briefs, surprisingly, is not addressed in the Bar Guide to Good Practice, although the *Code of Conduct for the Bar* states that counsel has a personal responsibility to ensure that a brief is not returned without the consent of the instructing solicitor (para. 506). The 1994 Report of the Bar Standards Review Body made various recommendations to reduce the number of returned briefs, but as a result of the introduction of automatic plea and directions hearings in all cases starting in 1995, it has been forecast that the phenomenon of returned briefs will 'increase hugely' (Zander 1994).

The Crown Court Case Preparation Package, a computer disk containing word-processed files with standard language for inclusion in prosecution briefs, was amended at the end of 1994 in order to cover child abuse cases. One option addresses the problem of briefs returned at the last minute by prosecution counsel:

> Every effort should be made in listing the case to ensure that counsel will be able to represent the prosecution at each hearing. In the event of a situation arising which necessitates counsel's withdrawal . . . counsel is requested to give the maximum possible notice in order to allow sufficient time for other suitably experienced counsel to be instructed, thus reducing the likelihood of any prejudice to the welfare of the child victim/witness.

EIGHT

TAKING ACCOUNT OF THE CHILD'S INTERESTS IN THE PROSECUTION PROCESS

Two initiatives were recently introduced to improve service to child witnesses. In 1993, the government endorsed the preparation of children to give evidence through publication of the *Child Witness Pack*, a joint initiative of four government departments and five children's organisations. In addition, the Lord Chancellor's Department asked each Crown Court to nominate a child liaison officer to provide a focal point for coordination with other agencies on a case-by-case basis. (This role is further described in chapter 9.) The glossy cover of the *Child Witness Pack* states that the children's books it contains are:

> designed to be read with an adult who is familiar with court procedures and can answer any questions the child may have. This adult will also be responsible for assessing a particular child's needs and passing this information to the police, Crown Prosecution Service and court staff.

The Pack was accompanied by a Joint Letter from the Home Office and other sponsoring government departments which described the person carrying out these functions as the 'independent adult'. However, there continues to be confusion about who may perform this role, and no government resources have been allocated to the work or training of 'independent adults'. In the criminal courts there is no equivalent to the funded position of guardian *ad litem* who is appointed by the court to represent the child's interests in civil care proceedings. (For arguments in favour of the extension of the guardian's role to criminal proceedings, see Whitcomb 1988; Plotnikoff 1990; Morgan and Williams 1992.) It must therefore be emphasised that there is still no one in the criminal justice system with official responsibility for representing the child's interests to the court, a role often mistakenly attributed to counsel for the prosecution.

Nevertheless, some policies take account of the child's interests in relation to specific issues, although with differing degrees of emphasis. This chapter contrasts the roles and responsibilities of the police and the CPS in this respect. In deciding whether to prosecute, police child protection units (CPUs) give a higher priority to the child's welfare than is possible under current CPS policy which states that the best interests of the child should be the first – but not the final – consideration when assessing the public interest.

In contrast to the different weight attached to children's interests in relation to the decision to prosecute, official statements are clear that the welfare of the child is paramount when deciding about the disclosure of information from the prosecution to care proceedings, or about whether a child should receive therapy pre-trial. Even so, these policies are often unknown or misinterpreted.

Notice of transfer provisions in the Criminal Justice Act 1991 place a duty on the Director of Public Prosecutions to certify that the case should proceed without delay at the Crown Court 'for the purpose of avoiding any prejudice to the welfare of the child' (s. 53(c)). This certification makes the provision of information about the child's interests even more significant. The CPS is given little information on which to base this or other decisions affecting the child's welfare.

This chapter, like the previous one, refers to a range of sources for CPS policies. We have distinguished those which are internal and therefore have confidential status, and those which are published.

THE DECISION TO PROSECUTE: THE ROLE OF POLICE CHILD PROTECTION UNITS

The government guidance *Working Together* gives equal weight to three factors in deciding whether child abuse cases should be prosecuted:

(a)   Is there sufficient substantial evidence?

(b)   Is it in the public interest that proceedings should be instigated against a particular offender?

(c)   Is it in the interests of the child victim that proceedings should be instituted? (para. 4.12)

Some police CPUs go further and state that 'the welfare of the child is of paramount importance and transcends all other issues as to whether it is in the child's interests to proceed [to prosecution]' (for example, the Metropolitan Police Child Protection Manual).

Working Together suggests that the basis of decision-making about criminal proceedings has broadened, at least where CPU officers and social workers are involved jointly. An expectation has been created that social workers will contribute to the decision to take criminal proceedings. For example, the *Memorandum of Good Practice* states that it 'builds explicitly on the Butler-Sloss and *Working Together* approach and is compatible with it' and emphasises 'the need to take full account of all the circumstances of the case *and the views of other agencies* before deciding that criminal proceedings will be appropriate' (p. 2, emphasis added).

The circumstances of the offence against the child may give rise to a child protection case conference. These inter-disciplinary meetings convened by social services are the formal process by which a decision is made to put the child's name on the child protection register. If the meeting is convened before a decision about criminal proceedings is made, its members may comment informally on the decision whether to charge. The weight given to participants' views may depend on the nature of inter-agency relationships. In order to provide geographical consistency across one large area, a central police unit attended all case conferences and controlled the provision of police information to the conference. Social services personnel commented that, because CPU investigating officers did not attend, 'nuances of information' may be lost. Nevertheless, here as in other areas the case conference could comment informally on the question of criminal proceedings.

It was pointed out by police and social workers that the views of participants did not necessarily follow a predictable or consistent path. Sometimes social services wanted the suspect to be charged but the police declined. In one area the police acknowledged that they so rarely had sufficient evidence to charge alleged abusers that, when it was available, they usually proceeded irrespective of social services' views.

Interviews sometimes indicated tension between the police and CPS about their respective policies and practice. For example, CPU officers in one police force thought that the CPS accepted less than half the cases put forward. They expressed concern that their local prosecutors operated unwritten rules, for example not pursuing cases of child witnesses under seven, although they were assured that decisions were dealt with on a case-by-case basis. They felt that the CPS looked for a higher standard of proof than was necessary, and that younger children were not considered as witnesses as often as was appropriate.

THE DECISION TO PROSECUTE: THE ROLE OF THE CROWN PROSECUTION SERVICE

The Prosecution of Offences Act 1985 gives the CPS responsibility to review and, where appropriate, conduct all criminal prosecutions (s. 3(2)(a)). There are two stages in the decision to prosecute. *The Code for Crown Prosecutors* (a published document) requires that, first, there should be a realistic prospect of conviction. Only then does the prosecutor consider the second test, whether a prosecution is in the public interest.

In 1991, the government agreed to be bound by the United Nations Convention on the Rights of the Child. Article 3.1 states, 'In all actions concerning children, whether undertaken by public or private social welfare institutions, courts of law, administrative authorities or legislative bodies, the best interests of the child shall be a primary consideration.' This contrasts with the 1992 version of *The Code for Crown Prosecutors* which stated that prosecution is 'almost always considered to be in the public interest in the case of sexual assaults against children' (para. 8). The 1994 edition of the Code has dropped this statement, although internal confidential guidance now advises that it will be rare in any child abuse case in which there is enough evidence for a realistic prospect of conviction for a prosecution not to be needed in the public interest, subject always to the primary consideration of 'the best interests of the child'.

The explanatory memorandum published along with the 1994 Code states that sexual assaults involving children are always serious offences and the CPS is committed to ensuring that 'appropriate action' is taken (para. 5.2). The Code identifies common public interest factors in favour of prosecution as including the victim's vulnerability, any 'marked difference in age between the actual or mental ages of the defendant and victim' and the defendant's position of authority and trust (para. 6.4). Public interest factors against prosecution include the likely effect of prosecution on 'the victim's physical or mental health, always bearing in mind the seriousness of the offence' (para. 6.5).

The 1992 *Memorandum of Good Practice* states that, 'In deciding whether to include a child's evidence, and whether it is in the public interest that a case should be brought to trial at all, the CPS will take into account the interests and wishes of the child' (para. 2.15). It goes on to say that reports to the CPS should include information about the wishes of the child and his parents or carers about going to court, but does not specify that the child's interests should be addressed. Nevertheless, police officers and social workers communicating with the CPS about the child need to provide both categories of information. The explanatory memorandum issued with the 1994 *Code for Crown Prosecutors* calls for consideration of the effect of prosecution on the victim in question. It directs prosecutors to distinguish between the victim's 'interests' and 'views', as the former are considered to be far more objective. Prosecutors need to be aware of the victim's views about what should happen in a case, but it is the victim's interests which should be considered in the wider public interest context. Nevertheless, although the victim's interests are important, they cannot be the final word on the subject of prosecution (paras. 4.28, 4.41).

CHILD WELFARE CONSIDERATIONS IN RELATION TO OTHER DECISIONS

The following table compares the position regarding the decision to prosecute, discussed above, with the weight attached to the child's welfare in other decisions. It is accorded 'paramount' or 'prime' importance in policies relating to the police decision to charge, the disclosure of information from the prosecution case to child protection proceedings and in deciding that the child should have therapy even though a prosecution is contemplated.

Child welfare considerations in decision making

DECISION	POLICY	SOURCE	COMMENT
Police decision to initiate criminal proceedings	'the welfare of the child is . . . paramount'	For example, Metropolitan Police Child Protection Manual	May not apply to decisions made by officers outside Child Protection Units
CPS decision to prosecute	'the CPS will take into account the interests and wishes of the child' the CPS 'must always think very carefully about the interests of the victim' when making public interest decision	*Memorandum of Good Practice on Video Recorded Interviews* *Code for Crown Prosecutors*	There is no standard mechanism for providing this information to CPS
CPS response to request to disclose information to civil care case	'The welfare of the child is of paramount importance'	CPS restricted policy statement	The policy is explained by the CPS to those who enquire
Decision as to whether child receives pre-trial therapy	'The needs of the child are of prime importance'	*Working Together*	Not reflected in written CPS policy until September 1994

No official publication sets out all these policies in a single document, and the distinctions between them are not always well understood by practitioners. This can give rise to misunderstandings about the agencies' respective roles.

COMMUNICATION BETWEEN THE POLICE AND THE CPS ABOUT THE CHILD'S WISHES AND INTERESTS

The *Memorandum of Good Practice*, which states that the CPS will 'take into account' the interests and wishes of the child in the prosecution decision, continues:

> Reports to the CPS should always include clear information about the wishes of the child, and his or her parents or carers, about going to court. The CPS may in any event need to seek further information from the joint investigating team. (para. 2.15)

Notice of transfer provisions place a duty on the Director of Public Prosecutions to certify that the case should proceed without delay at the Crown Court 'for the purpose of avoiding any prejudice to the welfare of the child' (s. 53(c)). This certification makes the provision of information about the child's interests even more significant. Prosecutors said that, in order to make an informed decision about notice of transfer, they would need more information about the child than was currently provided, including updates about therapy.

Little information about children's wishes and interests or the prejudicial effect of delay was reflected in project cases. Despite the policy requirements for this type of information, there is no standard police form for transmission of information about the views of children and their carers about giving evidence or other reflections of children's interests, such as the manner in which the child would prefer to give evidence. In a few cases, the child's statement or that of the parent concluded with an indication of feelings about going to court, for example, 'I can't cope with the thought of going to court at the moment' (mother).

Police CPUs, because of their key role in inter-agency liaison, ought to be better placed than ordinary police officers to obtain background information and consider the child's interests in deciding whether to charge the suspect with a criminal offence. Only 18 of the post-Act CPS case files contained a written indication of the interests and wishes of the child. Fourteen of these were provided by CPUs.

The views of the child and the opinions of the carer, police officers and any social worker in the case about the child's wishes and interests were not routinely sought. Only four project cases reflected written requests from the

CPS to the police for information about the wishes of the child and carers about going to court. (This is based on written information in CPS files and here, as in relation to other questions, it is possible that information was transmitted orally.) These were instances where there appeared to be uncertainty in the mind of the prosecutor about proceeding, for example where there was no medical corroboration and the police officer in the case was asked to check with the complainant that she appreciated that at trial it would be her word against that of her father.

The prosecution appeared much more ready to request additional information from the police where there was a question about the child's credibility, for example:

> I should like to see in conference the officers with a detailed knowledge of the girls and the way in which they are likely to give their evidence. (Counsel's advice, which described one girl's statement as 'clearly a pack of lies'.)

> This is not a strong case as there was no recent complaint or medical evidence. We have asked the police to ascertain the view of social services about discontinuing, and about the credibility of the victim. (Brief to counsel; in this case the defendant was convicted after jury trial.)

Discussions with prosecutors revealed a certain amount of caution over whether, and in what circumstances, information about the child and carers' views should be elicited. They pointed out that in law children, like adult witnesses, did not have a choice about going to court, and it should not be suggested to them that it was an option. In contrast to the views of the CPU officers, who thought that the CPS operated unwritten rules in declining cases unnecessarily, a group of prosecutors expressed the view that the police filtered out inappropriately some cases which should be prosecuted, by telling children and families that the child did not have to give evidence. These prosecutors described cases being forwarded to CPS as only the tip of the iceberg. Discussing the obligation to take into account the child's interests they quoted the *Memorandum*. This states that although a child witness is compellable:

> [T]his means only that a child who is wanted as a witness in court could be ordered to attend. It does *not* mean that, where the child is a witness for the prosecution, the CPS will insist on including the evidence of a child in which it is known that a child has provided some information to the police. (para. 2.15, emphasis in the original)

They felt that the *Memorandum* failed to acknowledge that:

. . . it is really the CPS's case. Although I doubt if we would ever compel a young person, we will not always drop a case just because the child wants to. The public interest requirement is a fact of life. *The Code for Crown Prosecutors* requires us to continue. A bit of firm talking [to the child] may help. A lot of public interest decisions which should be made by us are being made by police CPUs.

In some study cases it was clear from a review of the papers that the child's extreme reluctance to give evidence was known in advance and finally affected the outcome of the case. For example, in one case the child indicated his refusal to give evidence, a position supported by the social worker. Counsel was aware of this but said the trial should proceed because a High Court wardship action had been adjourned to accommodate the criminal case. At trial, the child 'froze' on the TV link and the defendant was acquitted. In another case, the victim's mother had always refused to bring the child to court and the prosecution offered no evidence.

In a third case, a 15-year-old girl whose brother was charged with incest told the CPU officer and wrote to the CPS in the strongest terms that she did not want to go to court: 'I think that at least I should have a say whether I wanted it to go to court or not, but nobody has really asked me.' The prosecutor's response was sensitive to the girl's feelings and also explained about the CPS's wider public responsibility. The letter concluded with an accurate reflection of the legal position:

> The court case will now go on whether or not you want it to. This is not because we do not care about your feelings but because of the responsibilities that the law places on us. . . . We hope that you will come to court of your own free will and give your evidence. I ought to emphasise that we do have powers to make you come to court but I am sure you would rather we did not have to do this. . . . It might help you to feel better when you think that the decision to prosecute your brother has not been your responsibility but the responsibility of the police and the CPS.

After a conference with the counsel in this case, the prosecution approached the defence, after which a plea to indecent assault was accepted.

THERAPY

In 1988, Home Office Minister John Patten announced that child abuse prosecutions should be given greater priority by the criminal justice system, in part because 'it is imperative that therapy to remedy the damage done by abuse, which may have to wait until legal proceedings are completed, should be provided after the least possible delay' (Home Office news release, 18

February 1988). In 1992, endorsing the admissibility of videotaped interviews, Mr Patten said they 'may facilitate earlier therapy for the child' (Hansard 1307, 28 February 1992).

It is a common, though mistaken, view that therapy must be delayed until after the trial in case it jeopardises the prosecution by tainting the child's evidence. Responding in a television interview to a question about the effect of pre-trial delay on child witnesses, Michael Lawson QC replied, 'For the period of the delay they can't receive any sort of counselling or therapy because that gives rise to that unconscious change in the evidence, or the possibility of it' ('The Brief', April 1994).

Possible dangers of pre-trial therapy put forward by respondents in this research included therapy:

(a)   being seen as 'coaching' the child;

(b)   involving leading questions resulting in the child making further disclosures and requiring additional statements to be taken; and

(c)   making children appear 'too confident' to the jury.

The last is an argument sometimes used against pre-trial preparation of child witnesses and even use of the TV link. Davies and Noon cited prosecution and defence barristers who emphasised the value of the child's tears in convincing a sceptical jury, and commented, 'judged from the standpoint of law, to exploit a witness's vulnerability and stress for the benefit of achieving a conviction seems a somewhat dubious procedure' (1991, p. 135).

The question of therapy is surrounded by much confusion. During our research many instances arose of police and social workers indicating that pre-trial therapy was not possible 'because the prosecution would not allow it'. These opinions are an inaccurate reflection of the official position of the CPS. Internal guidance issued to staff in 1994 stated the CPS cannot prevent therapy from taking place but prosecutors need to be aware that the therapy may be thought to taint the evidence. Prosecutors are advised to request that they be informed if it is to take place, that they be told of its nature, and that the therapist maintains and preserves notes of the contents of the therapy. In relation to the question of therapy, prosecutors must consider the best interests of the child which are the primary consideration.

Working Together states that:

There will be occasions when the child's need for immediate therapy overrides the need for the child to appear as a credible witness in a criminal case. This needs to be weighed up and a decision made on the basis of the available knowledge. There should always be discussions with the CPS on the particular needs of the child, and the needs of the child are of prime importance. The agencies should cooperate in assessing what is required and pool their resources to meet the diverse needs of individual children. (para. 5.26.9)

The *Memorandum of Good Practice* advises that once a videotaped interview is complete, 'it should be possible for appropriate counselling and therapy to take place. It should become standard practice to inform the police and CPS about the nature of any such therapy in each case' (para. 3.44). It may be possible to mitigate some evidential problems by providing advice to the therapist. If the individual child's demonstrable need for therapy requires the CPS to consider abandoning the prosecution, this directly affects the prosecutor's duty to act in the public interest, making it all the more important that the CPS receives full information about the child's welfare.

Perceptions are confused not just about CPS policy but also about the purpose of therapy. In the case of a child who was six when assaulted but aged eight by the time he was due to testify at trial, a police officer wrote to the CPS asking if it would be possible to relist the case to an earlier date:

He cannot receive proper therapy until any court proceedings are concluded as this would confuse the child. The aim of therapy is for the child eventually to forget the incidents, something that at this time we clearly do not want. It is however essential that this child receives therapy as soon as possible.

There is a mistaken view that the absence of a videotaped interview is a barrier to pre-trial therapy. For example, the police CPU advised CPS that, 'because [the child's] disclosure was prior to the implementation of the Criminal Justice Act 1991, he has not received any counselling or help to overcome the trauma caused, which cannot start until the trial has concluded'.

In another case, the concerns of a social worker and GP about a 14-year-old girl were communicated to the CPS and to the court. The trial of her step-father was originally scheduled for March but was vacated. In the intervening months, the social worker reported that the girl, extremely distressed, had taken an overdose. The GP wrote to the police in September with copies to the court, saying that the delays were causing the girl 'the most distress and damage. I cannot emphasise strongly enough the importance of this case being dealt with rapidly and finally from the point of view of her mental health'. CPS records reflected that 'the girl cannot be spoken to about the incident because of interference with the evidence'. The girl eventually testified at her step-father's trial the following January, but the case collapsed after she had given evidence for five hours. Afterwards, the social worker acknowledged that an experience like this 'means that investigating officers and social workers are affected as to how they deal with future cases and how they talk to children about going to court. They feel a great deal more cautious'.

If therapy takes place and the prosecution proceeds, the question about what can be disclosed to the defence about it may still arise. The *Memorandum* advises that 'The defence may justifiably wish to know about both the nature and content of the therapy that has taken place before the child gives evidence in cross-examination' (para. 3.44). In one project case, a social worker was cross-examined about the therapy received by the child. In another, the social worker's disclosure of information about the therapy to the defence may have been inadvertent. She had written to the CPS about her work with a 10-year-old which had revealed the extent of his anxiety about giving evidence in court. Prosecution counsel requested that the social worker make a statement after taking advice from the local authority legal department. 'She will probably have to bring her records to court. We are bound to serve letters already received [by the prosecution] on the defence.' Because a judge's decision about disclosable material is not appealable, there is very little guidance from case law, although *R* v *K* [1993] Crim LR 281 seems to suggest that therapy which avoids reference to the subject of specific allegations made by the witness and his or her evidence will not be prejudicial to the criminal trial and will not be disclosable. This uncertainty may have an effect on decisions affecting the child's welfare, as in the case of a 16-year-old girl witness. Her social worker described her as 'very frail and fragile, with a mental age of 11. She will certainly find the trauma of giving evidence very trying'. Nevertheless, it was decided on advice of counsel that she should not be referred to a child psychologist in case this provided 'ammunition for the defence'.

Only four CPS case files indicated an awareness that the child had received pre-trial therapy. One of these commented that an extremely distressed child was now 'more confident'. In two other cases, the CPS had received a request for advice about therapy from the police. In one there was no reply on file, but in the other the response stated appropriately that the CPS needed to know only the nature and extent of treatment, and to be kept informed of progress.

LIAISON WITH SOCIAL SERVICES AND THE RELATIONSHIP WITH CARE PROCEEDINGS

Parallel prosecutions and civil care proceedings

Circumstances surrounding 20 of our 200 criminal prosecutions also gave rise to civil care proceedings. This may underestimate the proportion of parallel proceedings. Because the sample was restricted to cases eligible for notice of transfer (involving at least one child eye-witness who might have been required to give evidence) it excluded prosecutions for assaults on younger children – typically, 'battered baby' cases. Such situations are also likely to give rise to care proceedings.

Requests for disclosure of social services' records to criminal proceedings

The majority of documents in social services' files are confidential and subject to public interest immunity. Nevertheless, both the prosecution and defence may wish to obtain these records because of the possibility that they contain information which could jeopardise the prosecution. Social workers, police and prosecutors confirmed that requests for disclosure were being made more frequently, often for the first time at trial. The problem is not restricted to cases in which there are formal care proceedings but may arise in any prosecution where it is believed that the social services department holds information about the child.

In some cases the belated timing of the request or the content of the materials in question affected the conduct of the prosecution. For example, in one case pleas were accepted 'reluctantly' because social work records significantly weakened the case against one of two co-defendants; and in another, case conference minutes were handed over by prosecution counsel on the eve of trial as 'a price worth paying for not having an adjournment'. As one prosecutor stated:

> Make no mistake, increasingly both prosecutors and defence are applying to the judge for orders of disclosure, and orders are being made. Children not involved with social services do not have their lives documented and risk disclosure in the same way. (Acting Branch Crown Prosecutor, speaking at British Agencies for Adoption and Fostering Legal Group Seminar, 26 May 1993)

When the question of disclosure of social services' records is raised at the last minute before trial, it usually necessitates lengthy legal arguments while the child is waiting to give evidence and may even cause adjournments, sometimes for the local authority to obtain representation. None of the fieldwork areas had a standard inter-agency procedure for dealing with disclosure, though initiatives are being taken elsewhere. For example, Cambridge CPS and the County Council legal department have developed a draft protocol which aims to avoid delays on the day of trial caused by last-minute requests from the defence and CPS for social work records.

Social workers were concerned that:

(a)   Education records are now being sought in addition to social work records.

(b)   Other agencies may be reluctant to provide material to assist social services because of the uncertainty over confidentiality.

(c)   Parents have no protection against self-incrimination at a child protection conference and should perhaps either be excluded or warned of this danger, though this puts a limitation on the use of the conference.

(d)   Social workers should be more aware of the potential vulnerability of their records.

(e)   Although requests for disclosure may be framed as concerning the defendant, they invariably relate to the children.

Requests for disclosure from the prosecution to care proceedings

Interviews with senior social workers highlighted tensions over the issue of disclosure of criminal records to care proceedings. Because CPS policies are not published, the social workers were unaware that the CPS approach to this question is extremely flexible. The following summary was provided by the CPS Policy Group: '[T]he welfare of the child is of paramount importance. . . . Even in cases where a risk to the success of criminal proceedings is identified it may still nevertheless be necessary in the interests of the child for disclosure to be given.' Although it is not usual for the CPS to disclose material before criminal proceedings are completed, in child care proceedings disclosure may be made before the criminal case is over.

NINE

THE RESPONSE OF THE CRIMINAL JUSTICE SYSTEM: THE COURTS

The courts received unequivocal directions, in the Victim's Charter 1990 and in the Criminal Justice Act 1991, that child abuse cases should be given priority. At the time our study was conducted, this was not incorporated into the Lord Chancellor's Department *Guidelines for Crown Court Listing* and was not reflected in the deliberations of judicial policy makers until 1993. Chapter 5 revealed that study cases took longer to reach disposition than the national average. We failed to identify any measures in fieldwork courts to monitor how long this class of cases took to reach disposition.

This chapter describes problems at magistrates' courts regarding the use of screens for child witnesses and, in a small number of cases, with the prosecution continuing to call children to give evidence at old-style committal proceedings when the law no longer requires their appearance in person.

A number of issues are discussed concerning the Crown Court: the identification of child abuse cases on receipt, the allocation of cases to the appropriate category of judge, listing (the scheduling of cases for hearing), the briefing of prosecution counsel, the use of TV links, screens and videotaped interviews for children's evidence, and the responsibilities of Crown Court child liaison officers.

We identified several factors with the potential of contributing to Crown Court delay. These included procedures for judge allocation and the policy of giving child abuse cases a fixed trial date which often meant booking court time many months ahead. (Following our research, the latter policy was amended to emphasise the priority to be given to child abuse cases.) Final hearings were often postponed. There was usually no continuity of judges handling pre-trial and trial matters in the same case. In over half of Crown

Court trials, the CPS was not represented by the barrister it had originally briefed. Case records reflected little sense of urgency on the part of judges, listing officers or the prosecution.

Despite a substantial financial investment by the Lord Chancellor's Department in TV link equipment, in study cases screens were used more frequently to shield children in the courtroom. The TV link was used in only 16 out of 41 trials in which children gave evidence at courts with these facilities. The pattern of usage was heavily influenced by local practice, suggesting that decisions about how children should give evidence were largely governed by the preference of lawyers and judges.

THE RESPONSIBILITY OF COURTS TO GIVE PRIORITY TO CHILD ABUSE CASES

The *Victim's Charter* published by the Home Office in 1990 states that 'The volume of business going through the courts means that priorities have to be set. Some of these are quite plain. An allegation of child cruelty or sexual abuse will always be given high priority' (p. 27). The Criminal Justice Act 1991 placed a statutory duty on the courts to avoid prejudice to the welfare of the child witness occasioned by unnecessary delay when notice of transfer is issued by the prosecution to move a case directly from the magistrates' court to the Crown Court (sch. 6, para. 7). Nevertheless, none of the fieldwork courts logged child abuse cases with a view to monitoring how long they took to disposition.

MAGISTRATES' COURTS

The management of child abuse cases

No directions about implementing the speedy progress policy for the prosecution of child abuse have been specifically addressed to magistrates' courts.

Visits were made to four magistrates' courts in different fieldwork areas and discussions were held with the clerk to the justices, senior clerk or listing officer. They saw their role as essentially responding to requests from the parties for court dates, and were not aware of particular problems of delay in relation to child abuse cases. None of the courts:

(a)   routinely received notice from the police or prosecution of cases involving children;

(b)   had a member of staff with special responsibility for child victim or witness cases;

(c)   had a policy of giving priority to child abuse or child witness cases, whether in listing court appearances, preparation of committal papers or transmission of files to the Crown Court;

(d)   monitored how long child abuse cases took to progress through the magistrates' court;

(e)   flagged their own case files as 'child abuse' or 'child witness', or identified them as such when forwarding case papers to the Crown Court.

The statutory period for despatch of papers from the magistrates' court to the Crown Court is four days (Magistrates' Courts Rules 1981 (SI 1981 No. 552), r. 11(2)). Some prosecutors reported routine delays of a week or more. The frequent failure of magistrates' courts to meet the four-day target has been described as causing a 'long-standing obstacle to expeditious listing in some Crown Courts' (Seabrook 1992, para. 319).

Courtroom screens for child witnesses

Magistrates' court staff said they were often made aware of child abuse cases only when they received a request for screens to be placed between the child witness and the defendant while the child gave evidence. (TV links are not available when a child gives evidence in a magistrates' court summary trial, though their use has, anomalously, been extended to youth courts.) Requests for screens were problematic if insufficient notice was given, as some courtrooms were more suited to their use than others and needed to be reserved in advance. The screens themselves were sometimes of an *ad hoc* nature. Mobile office partitions were commonly used, but were cumbersome and hard to manoeuvre in smaller and otherwise more appropriately informal courtrooms. Even custom-built screens integral to the courtroom design were sometimes completely unsuitable for the purpose. In one such court we observed a child's evidence disrupted several times while lawyers moved to different locations round the courtroom in order to try to see her in the witness-box which was curtained off. The child was visible only from the bench and the final placement of the participants involved the lawyers sitting on the bench to question her.

Old-style committals

At magistrates' court committal proceedings, the justices decide whether there is enough evidence to send the case to the Crown Court for trial. The majority are 'paper' committals which no witnesses need attend. An 'old-style' committal is a contested proceeding at which witnesses give live evidence, or at which the evidence is read from statements. Live testimony at committal is sometimes seen by both sides as a way of assessing whether witnesses come 'up to proof', in other words how they withstand cross-examination. Prior to the Criminal Justice Act 1991, the defence could require children to give evidence at 'old-style' committal proceedings as well as at trial in the Crown Court. In addition to being a further source of stress to the child, this gave the defence an opportunity to use the child's evidence at committal to challenge later, inconsistent testimony at trial. In pre-Act study cases, a total of 31 children gave evidence at committal proceedings in 18 cases. If it is anticipated that a magistrates' court hearing will last more than one day, whether for old-style committal or trial, it may be difficult to assemble a bench of magistrates who can sit on consecutive days. Thus in at least one project case, the child gave evidence at committal over two days, two weeks apart.

Section 55 of the Criminal Justice Act 1991 repealed s. 103 of the Magistrates' Courts Act 1980, which gave the defence the right to make the prosecution produce the child witness at committal. The amendment is limited to cases involving sex, cruelty or violence. (The age limits which apply are the same as in notice of transfer procedures described in chapter 7.) As Spencer and Flin (1993) have pointed out, 'if the legendary Fagin were prosecuted for intimidating a gang of children to make them steal . . . he could still insist on their making a live appearance at committal proceedings' (p. 87).

In law, the prosecution may now require a child to give evidence at an old-style committal only for the purpose of establishing a suspect's identity (Magistrates' Courts Act 1980, s. 1(b)). Nevertheless, children were told to attend old-style committal proceedings in eight post-Act cases, though identity did not appear to be at issue. Seven children in four cases attended court; three of these children in two cases gave evidence. In four other cases, the children failed to attend the committal proceedings and as a result in two cases the defendants were discharged. In one of these cases the defendant was later re-charged; in the other, charges against the defendant were proceeded with in relation to adult victims only.

The Criminal Justice and Public Order Act 1994 abolishes committal proceedings and replaces them with a transfer procedure broadly similar to the existing transfer provisions. However, the Criminal Justice Act 1991, s. 53 notice of transfer procedures are retained and will continue to be available at the discretion of the prosecution to expedite child abuse cases.

THE IDENTIFICATION OF CHILD ABUSE CASES AT THE CROWN COURT

Staff interviewed at Crown Court centres included the clerk of court (chief administrative officer), listing officer (the person responsible for scheduling cases) and child liaison officer (a new position described later in this chapter). With the exception of notice of transfer cases, none of the four courts visited was alerted automatically to cases involving children by the police, prosecution or magistrates' courts. Identification of such cases soon after receipt depended on review by Crown Court personnel.

When a file is received from the magistrates' court, Crown Court staff read it for a variety of purposes, for example, identification of likely guilty plea cases (noting where there are admissions in the defendant's statement) or the number and type of witnesses. The speed and thoroughness with which new files were reviewed depended on the pressure of work. Cases involving offences which are, by definition, against children are easy to identify. Others are not necessarily obvious. A child may be a witness to a serious assault on an adult and the only reference to the age of the witness is in the heading of the child's witness statement. Courts which required the preparation of a case summary in all cases said they used this to note that a child was involved. The covers of court case files were sometimes marked 'child abuse' or 'child witness', but this did not happen systematically.

The fieldwork was conducted when Crown Court centres were in transition from the use of manual listing records to the CREST computerised listing system. The manual system relied on colour-coded listing cards which were displayed in wall racks in the listing office. These cards recorded key features of each case and its progress through the court, and were moved to different racks according to the stage the case had reached. Most courts attempted to highlight these cards in some way where a child was involved, particularly if there was an application for TV link equipment. A glance round the walls of the listing office would reveal the number of child witness cases marked with, for example, a red star or yellow band.

Two courts converted to the CREST system during our fieldwork and dispensed with listing cards. Some listing office staff felt that they had lost the ability to monitor child abuse cases previously available with the manual card system. CREST does not specifically require the involvement of a child witness to be recorded. However, one of the courts used a CREST facility to enter a line of information on the computer as a 'highlighted' case note, for example 'screens required – child witness'. It is not possible to conduct a computer search on this field to produce a list of cases involving a child witness. Listing staff complained that special category cases can therefore only be identified by scanning through all the cases – probably hundreds – in a list. All the necessary date information is entered into CREST, which would allow the length of child abuse prosecutions to be monitored if special category case reports were made available. This would, however, require modifications to the CREST system.

THE ALLOCATION OF CHILD ABUSE CASES TO THE APPROPRIATE CATEGORY OF JUDGE

Listing (the activity of scheduling cases for hearing before a judge in court) is carried out by court staff on directions issued by the Lord Chief Justice and by Presiding Judges for each circuit. The process is under the supervision of a resident judge at each Crown Court centre. It is an anomaly that judges have responsibility for listing but no management control of the court staff who carry it out (Plotnikoff and Woolfson 1993, pp. 108–11). One of the first tasks to be carried out by the Crown Court on receipt of the case papers is allocation of the case to an appropriate category of judge for final hearing. Cases are not usually allocated to the same judge throughout and other judges are likely to hear pre-trial matters.

Completed Crown Court cases in our study were dealt with at disposition as follows (the category of one judge at final hearing was unknown):

(a)   17 by High Court judges;
(b)   136 by circuit judges; and
(c)   five by recorders.

The fact that nearly all of these cases were dealt with by the senior judiciary is an indication of the seriousness of the offences. (Nationally, recorders and assistant recorders accounted for 28 per cent of all cases committed for trial (Judicial Statistics 1992, table 6.6).) Offences are divided by seriousness into four classes, and guidance as to whether cases in each class should be tried by a judge of the High Court, a circuit judge or recorder, or released (i.e. heard by a lower level of judge than that initially indicated) is provided in the Lord Chief Justice's directions (Allocation of Business within the Crown Court, 1 January 1988). These directions require that a case of rape or of a serious sexual offence of any class against a child, may be released by a Presiding Judge for trial only to a circuit judge approved for the purpose by the Lord Chief Justice. All courts implemented screening procedures in order to identify and allocate appropriate cases to these approved judges.

In the Northern Circuit, for example, the resident judge (the most senior judge stationed at each Crown Court centre) is required to consider all sexual offences against a child under 16. He may direct which judge hears the case, or, where he considers that a 'serious' sexual offence is involved, seek the directions of a Presiding Judge. If the latter's decision is sought, specific procedural steps must be followed. A summary of the facts must be prepared by the prosecution or the court 'setting out general information about the defendant and victim and brief particulars of the offence' and the summary and other relevant case papers are submitted to the resident judge. He forwards these papers to the Presiding Judge (usually located at a different court), together with information about the anticipated plea, the expected length of trial and his recommendation as to judge allocation (Northern Circuit Presiding Judges' Directions, January 1992).

Although there was considerable local variation in these screening and allocation procedures, the process was invariably time-consuming and un-monitored. Factors contributing to delay included:

(a)   Screening of new cases, a process which required resident judge or Presiding Judge review, was conducted periodically (sometimes only every two or three weeks) rather than on receipt of each case.

(b)   Police case summaries were requested through the CPS or the Crown Court police liaison officer on a case-by-case basis (a process that can take several weeks) instead of being supplied automatically in appropriate cases.

(c)   Responses took several weeks from Presiding Judges.

In response to our research, the Lord Chancellor's Department consulted the circuits about the effectiveness of their arrangements for the release of child abuse cases; the circuits responded that 'far from contributing to delays, the procedures in place were working well' (letter to the authors, 17 October 1994).

CROWN COURT POLICY AND PRACTICE IN LISTING CHILD ABUSE CASES

The 'listing history' of individual cases is the key to understanding much about pre-trial delay. It was not possible to analyse in detail the listing of study cases because CPS files do not contain all of the relevant information and only a small selection of Crown Court files were reviewed. Nonetheless, some important factors emerged.

The Lord Chancellor's Department has taken steps to encourage greater consistency of practice, and in 1993 issued the first national *Guidelines for Crown Court Listing*. However, the mechanics of listing continue to vary widely. The Working Group on Pre-Trial Issues acknowledged that the development of national guidelines for each stage of Crown Court proceedings is made difficult by the 'absence of any recognised step by step procedure for the listing of cases between committal and trial' (para. 276). In order to retain flexibility, courts use a combination of strategies which allocate varying degrees of certainty to the starting date of the trial. To summarise, only a minority of cases are given a fixture, that is a fixed date for trial. Most cases go through a 'warned' list procedure (sometimes more than once) in which parties and witnesses are put on stand-by for a one- or two-week period during which the case can be called in for trial at 24 hours' notice. Some trials, whose status is even more uncertain, are designated as 'floaters'. These provide a back-up should a vacancy arise on the day, for example because the defendant in a trial with higher priority on the list enters a guilty plea at the last minute. A floater that is not reached on the day falls out of the list and must be relisted; it may even go forward to the next warned list and be floated again, although this is contrary to official listing policy. These methods provide a degree of flexibility, giving the court a relatively steady flow of work in the face of uncertainty about the numbers of trials which will proceed.

It is undesirable for cases with child witnesses to experience the usual degree of uncertainty inherent in the listing process. The Working Group on Pre-Trial Issues drew attention to instances where child abuse cases were inappropriately placed on reserve or warned lists, and recommended that they should always be given fixed trial dates in the Crown Court (para. 326 and recommendation 137). The *Guidelines for Crown Court Listing* state that child abuse cases need a greater certainty about the hearing date and 'once such cases have been identified either by the listing officer and resident judge or by the prosecution or defence, then they should always be given a fixed trial date' (para. 8.6).

The responsibilities of the Crown Court child liaison officer (see below) include liaison to ensure fixture for trial within eight weeks of committal or notice of transfer. There is no time guideline within which the trial itself should take place, only that a trial date should have been allocated. Fixtures are appropriate where TV link facilities are to be used, as particular court-rooms need to be reserved (Standing Commission on Efficiency, *The Crown Court: A Guide to Good Practice: the Lord Chancellor's Department* (1990), para. 6.12). Courts are advised to make every effort to adhere to a fixture, with the qualification that even these are subject to the risk of preceding cases over-running (para. 5.1 (ii)). Only in the most exceptional circumstances will the court seek to change a fixture, and if either party requests that it be vacated, then the consent of the other party is supposed to be obtained and agreement reached on an alternative date before any reference to the judge by the listing officer (paras. 8.2, 8.3).

Many of the project cases were assigned fixtures. The *Victim's Charter* states that child cruelty or sexual abuse cases will always be given high priority (p. 27). The *Guidelines for Crown Court Listing* initially made no reference to this policy, or to the Crown Court's statutory duty for cases received under notice of transfer to avoid prejudice to the welfare of the child witness occasioned by unnecessary delay in bringing the case to trial (Criminal Justice Act 1991, sch. 6, para. 7). The *Guidelines* propose that slots should be kept available to dispose of custody cases within the required 'speedy trial' time limits. They do not advise keeping such slots available for child abuse cases. The practice of simply allocating fixtures to child abuse trials is actually likely to result in further delay. The *Guidelines* acknowledge 'if too many cases are listed as fixtures there will be a reduction in flexibility in day-to-day listing. . . . In the longer term, the result will be [that] the fixtures will have to be made at increasingly distant future dates . . .' (para. 8.4). This was true even in the 'fastest' of the fieldwork courts, where fixtures were often listed five or six months ahead.

In April 1994, in response to our preliminary findings, the *Guidelines* were amended to emphasise that child witness cases are to be given the earliest available fixed date. The listing officer was advised that this date may be changed only in exceptional circumstances (paras. 8.6, 12.3). Final hearings were rescheduled in 34 out of 66 cases ending in a Crown Court trial, some more than once. Thirty-one cases which ended in a guilty plea or withdrawal had also been rescheduled; some of these were 'cracked' trials in which a trial collapsed at the last minute.

During the research, CPS clerks sometimes voiced frustration that their requests to the Crown Court for fixtures, or their observation that cases were 'unsuitable for the warned list' were ignored. In 1992, the CPS office in one study area tried unsuccessfully to get the local Crown Court listing office to adopt the procedure used in a neighbouring Crown Court, by which the CPS would identify to the court child abuse cases or cases where a child was giving evidence, requesting that the court give the case a priority listing as well as a fixture. Certainly, the study sample contained several cases which were 'floaters', i.e. stand-by cases not assigned to a specific court or judge but held in reserve on the day they are called to court waiting for a vacancy to occur in the trial schedule. From the listing officers' point of view, the designation of cases as floaters meant that at least some would be tried earlier than otherwise was possible, or that (as often happens) a plea would be entered because the trial was imminent. CPS requests for fixtures were much more common than those for priority listings (see chapter 7), but even the latter were sometimes not acknowledged. For example, in the case of a 12-year-old victim where the CPS requested a priority listing in May, the court correspondence said the case was 'not to be listed at this court before November, at which point it may be moved to [a TV link Crown Court] if it cannot then get a listing here [a non-TV link court]'. It was unclear why an earlier decision could not be made about use of the TV link, and therefore about transferring the case to an appropriate court. In April 1994, the *Guidelines for Crown Court Listing* were amended to stress that the listing officer 'will need to be particularly aware where those witnesses to be called include children' (para. 3.4).

Many study cases were listed for pre-trial review or plea and directions hearings. However, it appeared that few opportunities were taken by judges or others (in so far as could be assessed from court and prosecution files) to express a need for urgency, for example to resolve issues of disclosure to the defence of social services' records, applications for TV links or screens, the admissibility of the videotaped interview, or pressing the defence to identify the witnesses required to attend the trial. Matters which could have been addressed earlier were often left for the decision of the trial judge. Listing officers expressed frustration when cases, listed for a pre-trial hearing before a judge so that a fixed trial date could be established in court, were adjourned after hearing with no trial date set. This failure to exercise control may be due in part to the lack of continuity of judicial involvement from pre-trial hearing to trial.

CROWN COURT CHILD LIAISON OFFICERS

In May 1992, the Lord Chancellor's Department issued internal instructions to each Crown Court centre with TV link equipment, directing that a member of staff be nominated to act as child liaison officer, and identifying a lengthy and detailed list of responsibilities. The scheme has now been extended to all other Crown Court centres. Each court should have a named officer, together with a named deputy, identified on any leaflet or information which goes to relevant bodies. The role is 'resource neutral' in that the named member of the Crown Court staff performs these functions in addition to normal duties. Many of those designated are listing officers, i.e. those responsible for scheduling cases. Listing officers are well-placed to ensure child abuse cases receive priority treatment, but they are probably the busiest members of court staff. The Lord Chancellor's Department describes the child liaison officer as a non-delegable responsibility, although 'it is possible and often desirable for individual tasks to be delegated. It was never intended that the child liaison officer carry out all these duties personally' (letter to the authors, 17 October 1994).

The child liaison officer's function is to promote the welfare of child witnesses when in contact with the Crown Court and to provide a focal point for liaison with other agencies on a case-by-case basis. The child liaison officer is to be consulted by the listing officer to ensure that the needs of the child are addressed, and to alert the child liaison officer to any potential application for the use of TV links or screens (*Guidelines for Crown Court Listing*, para. 3.4 as amended April 1994). Responsibilities include awareness of all TV link cases 'from receipt of committal or notice of transfer', although, as was noted in chapter 7, such applications are often not filed until much later. Where notice has been issued, the child liaison officer has:

> an active role in facilitating the swift progression of such cases through the courts (e.g. by the introduction of an informal timetable agreed with the resident judge and the listing officer) . . ... Such a timetable could include the listing of a plea and directions hearing in all child witness cases at a set number of weeks following committal or notice of transfer, if agreed between the chief clerk, listing officer and resident judge.

Other child liaison duties include being available to answer questions about facilities or court procedure from the child witness's support person; organising toilet facilities, refreshments and lunch time arrangements prior to the child's arrival at court; and being on hand to meet child witnesses and conduct them to the 'safe' waiting area where there is no possibility of meeting the defendant or anyone else who may cause the child distress.

Discussions were held with three child liaison officers within six months of their appointment. At that stage, none had developed a record-keeping system accounting for the cases for which they were responsible or for monitoring how long they took to progress through the court, though they had set up arrangements for children's visits pre-trial and on the day of court. The Lord Chancellor's Department advocates the preparation of a local information booklet with the name and phone number of the child liaison officer, a map of the local area and a plan of the court building indicating a side entrance for the child's use (if available), as well as other court-specific details. In several areas we have visited during the course of this and other projects, police officers and witness support groups have been unaware of the role or identity of the designated person at their court.

CHILDREN'S EVIDENCE AT CROWN COURT: THE USE OF LIVE TV LINKS OR SCREENS

The following table is drawn from completed Crown Court cases which came to trial, in some of which both screens and links were used.

Children's evidence at Crown Court

	Pre-CJA		Post-CJA	
	No. of children	No. of cases	No. of children	No. of cases
Fully bound	87	34	46	25
Total giving evidence	76	36	40	25
Applications for TV link	–	14	–	10
TV link used	16	8	9	8
Applications for screens	–	19	–	9
Screens used	24	13	14	9
Gave evidence in open court	6	5	8	6
Manner of giving evidence unknown	30	12	9	6

Applications for TV links or screens are made at the discretion of the prosecution. A copy should be sent to the defence solicitors who may object, in writing and with reasons, within 14 days. The decision whether the application should be granted is made by a judge. Although applications can be determined without a hearing unless the judge otherwise directs (Crown Court Rules 1992 (SI 1992 No. 1847), r. 23 A, in study cases the decision to grant the application was often not made until the day of trial. Some judges handling pre-trial matters expressed reluctance to make a decision binding the trial judge. This in turn influenced the prosecution in some cases to delay applications, for example in this brief to counsel: 'The Crown proposes to call a large number of child witnesses . . . I believe that the correct procedure is to apply to the court for screens at the beginning of the trial.'

Before the Criminal Justice Act 1991, which extended the use of the TV link to older children, study cases were committed to 10 Crown Court centres only half of which had TV link facilities. Twenty out of 36 trials in which children gave evidence took place at TV link courts, but the link was used only in eight of these cases. By October 1992, when the Criminal Justice Act was implemented, seven of 12 Crown Court centres dealing with study cases had TV link equipment. Twenty-one out of 25 trials in which children gave evidence took place at TV link courts, but the link was used in only eight.

Applications for the use of TV links were made in 59 study cases of which 24 proceeded to trial. In seven of these cases, applications were unsuccessful and the 19 children involved gave evidence with screens. A total of 25 children testified over the link in 16 cases. Fourteen children in 11 cases gave evidence in open court.

When links were first introduced, various policy documents took the view that they would ultimately replace the use of screens (see Morgan and Plotnikoff 1990, p. 191). However, screens were more common than TV links in both pre- and post-Act cases, with a total of 38 children giving evidence this way. Even where screens are used, the layout of some courts allows the child to be seen from the public gallery giving rise to the potential for intimidation. This is also a concern where the defendant, rather than the child, is screened.

No national comparison between the use of screens and TV links is possible. On 16 November 1992, John Taylor, Lord Chancellor's Department Parliamentary Secretary, responding to a Parliamentary Question about the use of screens at Crown Court centres over the previous three years, stated that the information had not been collected. However, Mr Taylor reported that TV links had been used in 128 cases in 1990, 155 cases in 1991, and 91 cases as of 16 November 1992. Since 1993, the Lord Chancellor's Department has required courts to report the use of screens, though these statistics are not routinely published.

The 1991 Home Office evaluation of the TV link observed 100 cases involving 154 children and concluded that, 'Two years after its introduction, the live link enjoys widespread acceptance among all parties who have experience of its use in the courtroom' (Davies and Noon 1991). There are two important points to note about the Home Office study. First, it was based on cases in which applications to use the link had already been made, and found that such applications were almost always granted. It was not intended to provide an overview of child witness cases in general and did not include those in which no application for the TV link is made. Secondly, although the views of judges and barristers were solicited and were mostly favourable, CPS staff were not included in the evaluation. Their views are important, however, because they are responsible for applications to use the link. Very few of the CPS personnel interviewed for this project were aware of the positive conclusions expressed by the Home Office evaluation.

In our study, most CPS lawyers and law clerks (even those in areas where the TV link was used more frequently) expressed the view that testimony over the TV link lessens the impact of the child's evidence on the jury, and felt this reflected the opinion of many prosecution barristers, some of whom have publicly expressed concerns about the use of TV links. CPS clerks sometimes gave a strong indication of their preference, for example, 'can the officer in the case let me know which would be best method [TV link or screens] for the child to give evidence? It was indicated to the court that we would use screens if at all possible'. Even where an application has been made, the position taken by counsel on the day of trial may differ. The likelihood of a late change of plan increases if there is a return of the prosecution brief, i.e. a change of barrister on the day of trial (see chapter 7).

In the case of a five-year-old, his mother requested the TV link to be used as otherwise, in her opinion, he would be totally incapable of giving his evidence in open court and in the presence of the defendant. The CPS brief to counsel suggested, 'It may be that counsel decides, especially since this boy is expected to be a good witness, not to use the link since this may reduce the impact of the boy's evidence on the jury. It may be felt by counsel that a screen is more than sufficient protection for this young boy'. Counsel responded, 'I agree with those instructing me that a link should be available but if possible I would like to do without it. This will only be decided at court'. At trial, the boy gave evidence in open court with the defendant screened. The defendant was acquitted.

Peter Joyce QC has pointed out that for advocates, TV link technology takes 'some getting used to'. Barristers, accustomed to being on their feet in court, do not necessarily feel comfortable examining a witness while seated in front of the TV monitor and camera. However, lack of familiarity is by no means the only source of reluctance. Michael Lawson QC has said, 'I find there is an advantage with the screen because of human contact between counsel and the witness. I can give them a "don't let me down and I won't betray you" look if I need to' (Rickford 1992). Stephen Leslie QC believes that live TV links may put the prosecution at a disadvantage and reduce the impact of a child's evidence: 'Even though the child is in the other room, the idea of a television removes some of the reality.' Sally Howes points out that it is easier to keep the child's attention when face to face in court. Peter Joyce QC feels that there is 'something missing' when the link is used: 'When a child is there in front of you, you can tell quite a lot from a shrug or hanging of the head. You don't get that with the television link.' Professor Graham Davies points out that these comments fail to acknowledge the trade off between the loss of immediacy to the jury and the potential increase in amount of information conveyed by the child (letter to the authors, 3 March 1994).

The 1991 amendments to the Criminal Justice Act 1988 extended the eligibility of young witnesses to give evidence by TV link in cases of sexual and violent offences. Nevertheless, TV link usage is heavily influenced by local practice. At the Central Criminal Court in London, where a combination of cameras and screens is sometimes used to keep the child in the courtroom, children gave evidence by TV link in only nine cases between 1990 and November 1992 (Parliamentary Question, 16 November 1992) compared with an estimated use of screens in about 100 cases in 1990 alone (Morgan and Plotnikoff 1990, p. 191). There is nothing in the Criminal Justice Act 1991, or in the Rules made under it, to indicate how the judge should exercise his discretion. Some judges interpret the TV link provisions very restrictively. Awareness of judicial preferences was often reflected in prosecution briefs and inhibited the making of applications, irrespective of the needs of the individual child witness. For example, one CPS clerk advised counsel that 'I have not applied for the TV link because the judge in this case will only allow its use in special circumstances and age is no reason'. (The child in question was 10 years old.)

At one major Crown Court centre in our study, out of 26 trials in which children gave evidence, only five applications were made to use the link. Two were refused. In a third case, it was granted but not used. The link was used twice. In this court, the resident judge had issued a direction requiring all applications for use of the TV link to be supported by a separate statement from the parent, carer or social worker as to why the child needed to give evidence this way. This direction, which was later extended to include evidence by videotaped interview, was issued without consultation with the police superintendent responsible for local child protection units. Although the police obtained the necessary statements (which may have had the effect of raising expectations about availability of the link), the resident judge's direction appeared to have a 'chilling' effect on local practice. It also had a significant impact on police and social work resources. As one prosecutor noted:

> This is an ongoing problem. The police child protection units have said they will try to obtain letters in support of applications for the videotaped interview and TV link well before transfer or committal in all cases. The police are, however, finding it virtually impossible to obtain anything from Social Services.

VIDEOTAPED INTERVIEWS

The Criminal Justice Act 1991 permitted a videotaped interview with a child to replace the child's evidence-in-chief, provided that the child was available for cross-examination at trial. Soon after its introduction, some confusion was apparent about the relationship of various provisions of the Act. For example, in one case, a police child protection officer wrote to the CPS to report that 'as none of the children were videotaped, it is not possible to make an application for the TV link'. This was a mistaken view but no application was made.

In the pre-Act study cases, 14 interviews had been videotaped but the law did not permit them to be shown to the jury in the event of a trial. After the Act, interviews were videotaped in 36 cases. Nine of these cases went to trial and the videotape was shown in three. These three trials took place at different Crown Court centres and all three resulted in acquittals. The impact of these cases could be greater than the numbers suggest. Where a new procedure is perceived to be unsuccessful because trials result in acquittals, participants may be reluctant to employ it in subsequent cases.

It has been anticipated that the admissibility of videotaped interviews will result in a higher rate of guilty pleas. It was too early for us to assess whether this is true; guilty pleas were entered in 20 videotaped interview cases, but seven other cases had not been completed. Prosecution files did not reflect whether videotaped interviews had been shown to defendants. It was evident, however, that in some cases videotapes were not disclosed to the defence until after pre-trial hearings in the Crown Court, and this contributed to delay in pre-trial preparation.

Variations in local practice surrounding the introduction of videotaped interviews emerged soon after the Act's implementation. Neither the Criminal Justice Act 1991, nor the relevant rules of court nor the *Memorandum of Good Practice* refer to the provision of a transcript of the videotaped interview's contents. Nevertheless, a number of courts required transcripts, raising resource questions about who should pay for production, and some police forces had refused to supply them. The need to comply with last-minute judicial orders for transcripts required some videotapes to be sent to external transcribers, incurring an undesirable security risk. Prosecution counsel were instructed to resist applications from the defence or suggestions by the judge that a transcript was necessary. These unresolved tensions contributed to delay. Speaking at a conference at the University of Leeds, the Presiding Judge of the North East Circuit, Mr Justice Holland, suggested that it might be necessary to abandon the use of videotaped evidence in order for trials to take place quickly (22 April 1994, 'A Charter for child witnesses?').

The technical and evidential quality of tapes was often questioned by the CPS. In one area, a senior officer in a police CPU wrote to the CPS to express his disappointment that:

from such an early date the prosecution seems to have a negative attitude towards the use of the video which could prevent some of the ordeal of trial. The Criminal Justice Act 1991 gives the court the power to reject the video recording and we should, in my view, not be seeking to take that decision away from them.

The CPS responded that there was not a realistic prospect of conviction based on the videotape in question and that the child should therefore be examined by prosecution counsel.

Another variation in practice concerned 'refreshing the child's recollection'. Speaking before the introduction of the Criminal Justice Act 1991, Minister of State John Patten said, 'seeing the video before he or she gave evidence would be a most useful way of refreshing the child's memory' (Hansard 1308, 28 February 1992; see also Spencer and Flin (1993), p. 417). Internal guidance issued by the CPS and Lord Chancellor's Department state that child witnesses see their videotaped interview at the same time as it is shown to the judge and jury. Any direct examination and cross-examination then follows immediately. This procedure does not take account of the short attention span of young children (particularly in the alien surroundings of the TV link room), or the likelihood that some children may be very distressed at seeing themselves talk about traumatic events after a long gap in time. In some areas, applications are made for the child to view the tape earlier; elsewhere we were told that 'the CPS would not allow it'. CPS headquarters advised us that videotapes should be treated like other statements. The child could view the video on the day before trial if appropriate, though not weeks before, and should not see it many times.

In all three trials in the study sample in which videotapes were shown, arrangements were made for the child to see the tape ahead of time. In one area, the police had developed a 'witness video pre-court viewing' form. Local policy required that the child's viewing of the videotape be supervised by the original joint interview team. The form recorded the date when the tape was made, the time and location of showing it to the child, the persons present, and comments made by the child while watching the tape. In the second case, prosecution counsel obtained the judge's leave for the child to view the video 'some time before' court. In the judge's opinion this was 'perfectly proper', but the CPS expressed concern to the police that it was 'not for us [i.e. the CPS] to arrange'. In the third case, the six-year-old was allowed to watch the videotape the day before the trial, though not while it was shown to the jury. Prosecution counsel stated later, 'with benefit of hindsight this was unnecessarily restrictive. It is desirable that the child sees the video as close as possible to the time of cross-examination'.

As with TV link applications, decisions about videotaped evidence are often deferred to the morning of trial. In one of the first trials in this country at which videotaped evidence was admitted, the judge withdrew the case from the jury. Prosecution counsel later wrote to the CPS:

> The procedure created by the Rules envisages these decisions being made in advance of trial at a time when the child is not present. This also allows sufficient time for the video to be edited if necessary. Decisions were made in respect of the video application while this six year old girl was waiting at court to give evidence. This was most undesirable and ought not to happen.

TEN

THE MANAGEMENT OF CHILD ABUSE PROSECUTIONS

The purpose of our study was to evaluate the government's policy, first stated in 1988 and incorporated into provisions of the Criminal Justice Act 1991, to give priority to child abuse prosecutions in the criminal justice system. Two hundred cases were monitored over a period of two years. By the end of the study, 186 had reached plea or trial. The research discovered that these cases, far from receiving priority treatment, actually took longer than the national average to reach disposition. Cases tried at the Crown Court took, on average, over 10 months from first appearance at magistrates' court to final hearing. New statutory procedures to expedite cases were little used and were ineffective in delay reduction. Cases where the new procedures were used actually took longer than others in the study sample.

This chapter discusses the characteristics of an effective system for managing child abuse prosecutions: clear definitions; availability of policy guidance; systematic identification of cases to which the policy applies; performance monitoring; accountability for policy implementation; coordinated case management; informed decision-making in relation to the child's welfare; and a structure for inter-agency liaison.

The chapter concludes with a discussion of more fundamental changes required if the criminal justice system is to become genuinely sensitive to the needs of children.

THE CHARACTERISTICS OF EFFECTIVE CASE MANAGEMENT

Clear definitions

The goal of case management is to achieve the just and speedy determination of cases before the court. Traditionally, courts process most cases the same way, and until recently only cases in which the defendant is in custody were assigned to a fast track. Despite the government's commitment to expedite child abuse cases, there is no clear understanding among practitioners of the categories of children's cases which should be given priority. In study cases, this undermined from the outset procedures for identification and monitoring.

At the end of 1994, the CPS issued an internal National Operational Practice Service Standard giving priority to cases defined as child abuse by the joint government publication *Working Together* covering neglect, physical injury, sexual abuse and emotional abuse. This definition covers a broader range of children than those covered by the more restrictive statutory limits of the Criminal Justice Acts of 1988 and 1991. The welfare of child victims who do not give evidence because of age or other reasons may be directly affected by the outcome of a criminal case, for example where care proceedings have been delayed as a result. It is right that such criminal cases should also be eligible for priority treatment.

A definition of cases to which the speedy progress policy applies must be produced and applied consistently across criminal justice system agencies. Such cases can then be placed on a fast track and monitored.

Policy guidance

The government commitment has not been translated into detailed guidance for each of the agencies involved explaining how the speedy progress policy is to be implemented. Although the *Guidelines for Crown Court Listing* were amended in 1994 to emphasise that child witness cases should be given the earliest available fixed date for trial, there is still is a dearth of information on how the policy should be implemented by judges.

Directions for magistrates' courts are needed which build on the recommendations of the Working Group on Pre-Trial Issues, requiring magistrates' courts to monitor the progress of individual cases and agree timescales with the prosecution and defence for the completion of pre-trial stages.

Crown Court centres should be required to monitor the progress of child abuse cases, in particular notice of transfer cases which the court has a statutory duty to expedite.

Guidance is needed which identifies ways in which judges can facilitate the speedy progress policy without jeopardising the interests of the defendant.

Statements interpreting various aspects of the speedy progress policy and child welfare considerations in criminal proceedings are scattered across different documents.

Relevant policies and procedures should be published collectively. There is an urgent need for a policy statement addressed to police, prosecutors, social workers and courts explaining that decisions relating to pre-trial therapy for the child witness must be based on the child's best interests, and that therapy cannot be forbidden by the prosecution.

Some of the most important policies are contained in internal CPS guidance which is not publicly available. However, the CPS took an important step in collecting and updating relevant procedures in September 1994, when it distributed 20 pages of policy and casework guidance to its staff about cases involving child witnesses. The National Center for the Prosecution of Child Abuse in the United States has developed a prosecutors' manual which is also used as a reference by other agencies and would be a useful model here. *Investigation and Prosecution of Child Abuse* (1993) contains sections on assessing validity, allegations involving multiple children and suspects, considerations when the victim is physically or mentally disabled, the child's testimony (including strategies when the child freezes or recants) and meeting common defences in child sexual abuse cases. The chapter on the dynamics of victimisation includes discussion of indicators of abuse, child development, delayed disclosure and recanting, issues with which prosecutors are not likely to be familiar.

Systematic identification of cases

The first requirement of a fast track system is a clear method of highlighting cases for inclusion. In the first year of our study, none of the police forces routinely marked or flagged files as child abuse when forwarding them to the CPS. National policy now requires that all cases be sent with a standard front sheet on which a 'special category' box is ticked. In the project's second year, 25 cases out of 60 in which the form was used were identified as 'special category'. This box is fairly unobtrusive and something more conspicuous would highlight case papers, both when handled internally and when in transit between agencies. Even if police papers are not flagged, CPS policy requires that its staff identify child abuse cases upon receipt. Of 200 study cases, only 51 CPS files were so identified. CPS files are put into different manila covers when the case progresses from the magistrates' court to the Crown Court. Sometimes one or other file cover was designated 'child abuse', but not both.

No magistrates' courts visited during the research flagged their own case files as 'child abuse' or 'child witness', or highlighted them as such when forwarding case papers to the Crown Court. With the exception of notice of transfer cases, which by their nature invoke a special procedure, none of the Crown Court centres visited was alerted automatically to cases involving children by the police, prosecution or magistrates' courts. After screening by court staff, some Crown Court files were flagged as child abuse, but these were not consistently the same cases identified by the CPS. The fast track process needs to take account of the fact that not all eligible cases are dealt with by police child protection units (CPUs).

A consistent inter-agency approach to case identification is the foundation of effective management of the speedy progress policy. The fast track designation should be allocated by the police soon after the offence is reported and stay with the case as it progresses through the system. Additional cases may be designated on receipt by the CPS, such as those which have not originated in a CPU. Colour-coded case files or face sheets would facilitate this process.

Performance monitoring

The *Victim's Charter* and the notice of transfer provisions of the Criminal Justice Act 1991 direct courts to give child abuse cases priority. In practice, study cases took significantly longer than the national average at magistrates' court and Crown Court. Cases consistently failed to complete key stages in the pre-trial process within the time limits recommended by the Working Group on Pre-Trial Issues (an inter-agency group chaired by the Lord Chancellor's Department). These recommendations define the time frames which the CPS acknowledges should be the targets for child abuse case management.

The process by which even a 'straightforward' child abuse case comes to court is highly complex, requiring the involvement of around 50 individuals in the criminal justice system. As a result it is argued that many factors contributing to pre-trial delay are outside the purview of the court or the prosecution. Nevertheless, it is unlikely that adequate attention will be given to those factors which are susceptible to control until there is recognition of the scale of the problem. There are no mechanisms in place to track the progress of these cases through the criminal justice system. This holds true even for cases subject to notice of transfer, the innovation introduced by the Criminal Justice Act 1991 specifically to reduce delay.

National monitoring is necessary in order to assess adherence to policy commitments. National statistics should be published. Criminal justice computer systems should be enhanced to provide both local and national management information.

Case progress with regard to the targets established by the Working Group on Pre-Trial Issues should be monitored by the police, CPS and the courts.

In 1994, the CPS issued the National Operational Practice Service Standard, 'According Priority to Child Abuse Cases'. This introduces for the first time a requirement that CPS Areas maintain records of the time taken to deal with child abuse cases. The measure selected is the time interval between charge by the police to final disposal, a period not used in other criminal justice system statistics. Areas have been told they need not maintain records of the nature of the final disposal. The Service Standard measure therefore fails to distinguish cases disposed of by discontinuance, offers of no evidence, withdrawal, judge directed or ordered acquittal, pleas of guilty and sentence, conviction and sentence, and orders for charges to lie on the file.

It is intended that the provision of average processing times between charge and disposal will:

> enable CPS headquarters to compare figures between Areas and thereby to monitor CPS performance as a whole. We intend to examine the figures critically with a view to spotting locations where there appear to be problems. If necessary, we will call for analysis of the figures in individual Areas. Thus the provision of returns to headquarters will be used as a warning signal. (letter from the Policy Group, 28 November 1994)

We have expressed the view to the CPS that a measure based solely on the interval between charge and disposal will not provide warning of problems. The absence of a breakdown by type of disposal is likely to skew average returns because of the high proportion of child abuse cases that go out of the system at an early stage.

The CPS has responded that it is not its function to produce national statistics, and the purpose of the Service Standard is to encourage local management 'to make a determined effort to give effect to the speedy progress policy for child abuse cases'. Responsibility for monitoring lies with local offices which are required to keep child abuse case registers, an existing requirement which was re-emphasised in an internal report circulated in July 1994 (letter from the Policy Group, 28 November 1994). The details to be recorded in these registers have not been specified by CPS headquarters. Our research suggested that the quality of the registers varies widely. The Service Standard requires local managers to ensure that 'the intervals between the key stages of the prosecution process are the minimum consistent with the completion of all relevant tasks for which the CPS is responsible'. The local registers we examined would not have served this purpose.

In order to facilitate CPS monitoring of the 'speedy progress' policy both locally and nationally, and to provide a basis for comparison with national Judicial Statistics, the CPS should record:

(a)   the date of first appearance in magistrates' court;
(b)   where appropriate, the date of committal or transfer (distinguishing notice of transfer cases);

(c)   the date and type of final disposal.

Accountability

Accountable systems identify those to whom responsibility has been delegated and incorporate management controls to monitor performance. Within the CPS, senior lawyers have responsibility to keep the progress of child abuse cases under constant review to prevent avoidable delay. According to the Lord Chancellor's Department policy, Crown Court child liaison officers have 'an active role in facilitating the swift progression of such cases through the courts' (May 1993 internal guidance). Many of them are also listing officers and are therefore well placed to monitor case progress. Nevertheless, neither they nor senior CPS lawyers are accountable for the implementation of the policy. Indeed, individuals fulfilling these roles in fieldwork areas did not receive reports which would enable them to monitor the progress of pending children's cases.

At a local level, those with responsibility for implementation and monitoring of the speedy progress policy should be clearly identified.

Coordinated case management: the pre-trial process

Fixed trial dates can be a source of delay because they often need to be set many months in advance. Requests for priority listings were made in only five study cases. Following our research, in 1994 the Lord Chancellor's Department amended its *Guidelines for Crown Court Listing* to reflect that child witness cases should be given the earliest possible fixed date for trial.

The CPS should routinely request priority listings, not just fixtures, from the Crown Court listing officer.
Crown Court listing officers should assign trial dates to fast track cases which combine the benefits of fixtures with a priority listing.
The Circuit Administrator and Presiding Judge should ensure that they are notified where no judge is available locally to try a fast track case. The Circuit Office should monitor court performance in disposition of these cases, including problems relating to availability of judicial resources.

The involvement of the same judge and barristers throughout the life of an individual Crown Court case is the exception rather than the rule. (And of course completely different personnel – magistrates, court clerks and CPS lawyers – deal with the case at the magistrates' court.) In order to maintain maximum scheduling flexibility, it is common for a different judge to handle the case each time it appears in court. In this situation, no judge has sole responsibility for managing its progress. The most serious cases, those tried by a High Court judge, are often the least likely to have judge continuity between pre-trial and trial.

Most cases appear in court at least once prior to trial for a hearing at which the defendant enters a plea, but these are often relatively cursory proceedings in which one or both sides is represented by 'stand-in' counsel. The *Crown Court Study* carried out for the Royal Commission on Criminal Justice found that the same judge handled the pre-trial hearing and the trial in 17 per cent of cases and that prosecution counsel were the same in only a third (1993, paras. 2.4.6 and 2.8.4). The Pre-Trial Issues Working Group found that the same judge was involved in both proceedings in only 6 per cent of cases; continuity of representation was provided by the prosecution and defence barristers in 8.5 and 21 per cent of cases respectively (1994, paras. 63, 120). Lack of judge and barrister continuity in the pre-trial stage contributes to poor case management and therefore to delay.

In just over half of our study cases in which a Crown Court trial was held, the trial date was rescheduled, sometimes more than once (this does not include rescheduled trials which 'cracked', in which a guilty plea was entered or the prosecution was withdrawn at the last minute). The Lord Chancellor's Department revised its *Guidelines for Crown Court Listing* in 1994 to state that trial dates in child abuse cases should be changed only in exceptional circumstances. Nevertheless, on the day of trial, judges may feel obliged to accede to an application for an adjournment in the interests of justice. In our study, it appeared that only the minority of rescheduled trials were necessitated by unforeseen circumstances. The majority of such applications seemed to be more the culmination of poor planning by the parties and inadequate pre-trial management by the court.

Judges at pre-trial hearings are often reluctant to make decisions which bind the trial judge, and as a result many decisions are put off until the morning of trial. The Royal Commission recommended that the trial judge be bound by any orders or rulings made by the judge who presides over the preparatory hearing. It also recommended that counsel for the defence and prosecution should be prohibited from seeking to reopen any matter decided at the pre-trial hearing (recommendations 147, 149). For fast track children's cases, issues to be resolved ahead of trial include applications for use of the TV link or screens, the admissibility of a videotaped interview and questions concerning disclosure of social services' records. We found that these decisions were often made on the morning of trial, sometimes while the child waited to give evidence.

There are two types of pre-trial hearings at which matters can be resolved in advance of trial. At a plea and directions hearing the defendant enters a plea, and if this is 'not guilty' the judge may rule on certain matters in relation to the trial. It is described by the Working Group on Pre-Trial Issues as 'a short, sharply focused hearing for use in the generality of cases'. Following a pilot study, in 1994 the Working Group recommended that in order to encourage early case preparation, magistrates' courts should be able to schedule all cases for a plea and directions hearing in the Crown Court on a specific date. This recommendation, which includes provision of a standard checklist for judges, is to be phased in nationally beginning in January 1995. However, not all matters can be resolved at this type of hearing which should be held soon after receipt at the Crown Court. Adequate time may need to be set aside for a more in-depth pre-trial review, particularly where video-taped evidence is to be played.

The Royal Commission speculated that it may require a change in the law to empower the judge at a pre-trial hearing to make decisions which bind the trial judge (p. 107). If such decisions cannot now be made binding, then greater consideration needs to be given to ensuring that the trial judge is available to handle specific pre-trial matters in contested cases. The Commission recommended that where,

> disclosure, severance or the admissibility of evidence is particularly sensitive and likely to be of critical significance, the trial judge should be nominated as soon as the CPS have alerted the court to the situation and should take over the management of the case from that point right through to the conclusion of the trial. (recommendation 148)

One possible model is the procedure applied in complex fraud trials (the category in which the by-passing of committal proceedings also originated). In such cases, s. 8 of the Criminal Justice Act 1987 provides that the trial begins with the preparatory hearing. The *Guidelines for Crown Court Listing* were amended in April 1994 to provide that in s. 8 cases, 'the judge presiding at the preparatory hearing must be the judge who, except in exceptional circumstances, conducts the trial' (para. 11a).

Following the recommendation of the Scottish Law Commission, in 1990 the Lord Justice General of Scotland issued a memorandum containing a checklist of child witness issues 'to provide assistance to judges in the exercise of their discretionary powers' with the 'general objective . . . to ensure, so far as is reasonably practicable, that the experience of giving evidence by all children . . . causes as little anxiety and distress to the child as is possible in the circumstances'.

A practice direction should be developed providing a checklist of issues which could be resolved in advance of trial, distinguishing those issues which can only be decided by the trial judge.

The court listing office should schedule, wherever possible, a pre-trial hearing before the trial judge in fast track cases, ensuring that enough time is allocated to

deal with the matters at issue and that facilities are available if necessary for the
playing of videotaped evidence.

Judges at pre-trial hearings in fast track cases should be prepared to exercise
greater control by anticipating and dealing with questions which may 'derail' the
trial date (typically in relation to witness requirements, medical experts, video-
taped evidence and disclosure of social work records). This would enable the court
to take a more robust view of requests to vacate fixed trial dates.

The process by which the trial judge is allocated is itself a potential cause
of significant delay. Crown Court cases are classified by seriousness of offence
for allocation to the appropriate category of judge at final hearing. Although
there is considerable local variation in screening and allocation procedures,
we found that the process was invariably time-consuming and unmonitored.
However, we have been advised by the Lord Chancellor's Department that
the circuits describe procedures for the release of cases as 'working well'
(letter, 17 October 1994).

Procedures for the allocation of judges to cases, a potentially significant source
of delay, need to be monitored. Systematic identification of fast track cases would
permit:

(a)   screening of new cases requiring review by the resident judge or Presiding
Judge to be conducted on receipt rather than periodically;
(b)   police case summaries to be supplied automatically in appropriate cases
rather than requested through the CPS or Crown Court police liaison officer on a
case-by-case basis (a process that can take several weeks);
(c)   the monitoring of time taken by resident judges and Presiding Judges to
make allocation decisions.

Coordinated case management: the responsibility of the CPS

Many CPS areas attempt to brief counsel with some degree of expertise in child
witness cases. Some offices now try to take this further by monitoring counsel's
performance and not briefing them again where it is unsatisfactory. Barristers
suggested to us that more should be demanded of them, for example the CPS
should require counsel to be familiar with the *Memorandum of Good Practice on
Video Recorded Interviews*. However, in just over half of the Crown Court trials in
the study sample, first briefed prosecution counsel did not appear at the final
hearing. When a substitute barrister takes on the case at the last minute, the
opportunity for preparation and liaison is curtailed. The new counsel may take a
different view of the strength of the case or how the child should give evidence.

The Crown Court Case Preparation Package is a computer disk containing
word-processed files which provide optional standard paragraphs for

incorporation into prosecution briefs according to the requirements of the case. Standard language specific to child abuse cases was not used at the time our research was conducted, although the study identified a number of areas in which instructions to counsel did not follow through on particular prosecution policies. At the end of 1994 the Case Preparation Package was amended to incorporate optional language relating to child abuse cases.

Only one brief in our sample advised counsel to 'resist delay'. The National Operational Practice Service Standard issued by the CPS to senior managers in 1994 requires that counsel be notified in instructions of the importance of according priority to child abuse cases. The Case Preparation Package now includes standard language instructing counsel to 'use his or her best endeavours to fix an early trial date and to resist any attempts to delay the listing of this case'. Counsel may be advised:

In all cases involving children (whether as victim or witness), the best interests of the child are a primary consideration. As counsel will appreciate, the trauma suffered by the child may be minimised if the period during which an impending case is hanging over a child is kept as short as possible. This would also reduce the risk of the case being lost through impairment of the child's memory.

Counsel may also be instructed that specific attention be given to the scheduling of child witnesses' testimony.

The approach of counsel to child witnesses before court varies widely. Some make a point of introducing themselves beforehand; others refuse to do so. In 1994, the Bar Council voted to abolish the rule in its Code of Conduct restricting barristers' contact with witnesses. It agreed to draw up guidelines enabling barristers 'to reassure victims of crime and other vulnerable witnesses and to discuss evidence with witnesses when this is necessary in the interests of justice' (press release, 29 November 1994).

The cover of briefs to counsel in child abuse cases should emphasise their priority status.

Standard instructions to counsel in child witness cases should:

(a)   address the introduction of prosecution counsel to the child witness;

(b)   emphasise the resolution of as many issues as possible in advance of trial, including how the child is to give evidence.

Applications for use of the TV link are required to be made within 28 days of committal. In almost half of the study cases, the prosecution made applications out of time, on average 76 days after committal. Delay was often due to the CPS waiting for an indication of plea from the defendant, clarification of the child's witness status or (in the court where this was required by the resident judge's practice direction) receipt of a statement in support of the application from a social worker. Late applications made it more likely that decisions about use of the TV link would be deferred until the day of trial and in a few cases necessitated transfer to other courts, a process which itself generated delay.

> *Before committal or transfer, consideration should be given to the need for TV link facilities so that the case can be assigned to the appropriate court, early applications made, and judges requested to rule on the application after receipt of the defence's response well in advance of trial.*

Notice of transfer procedures are the first attempt to give legislative status to the speedy progress policy for child abuse cases. Introduced by the Criminal Justice Act 1991, these procedures give the prosecution the discretion to move certain categories of child witness cases directly to the Crown Court by avoiding committal at the magistrates' court. In our study, notice of transfer was used in only 11 cases in two out of the five study areas. Notice was often issued as a response to the defence electing Crown Court trial. The few completed notice of transfer cases actually took longer at Crown Court than other cases in the study sample. Guidance issued to CPS staff in 1994 has placed greater emphasis on the use of notice of transfer procedures, emphasising that they 'shall' be used unless jurisdiction has been retained by the magistrates' court or the defendant faces a number of indictable offences, only some of which qualify for s. 53 procedures.

> *In accordance with CPS guidance, greater consideration should be given to issuing notice at an earlier stage prior to the mode of trial decision in the magistrates' court. Notice of transfer cases should be monitored to ensure that these cases are actually given priority in the system.*

Informed decision-making concerning the child's welfare

The *Memorandum of Good Practice* emphasises the need for investigators to take full account of all the circumstances of the case and the views of other agencies before deciding that criminal proceedings are appropriate. If the case is referred to the CPS, prosecutors are required to consider both the child's views and interests. Some of the prosecutors to whom we spoke were cautious as to whether information about the child's and carer's views should be elicited at all, and indeed the CPS is directed to give greater emphasis to the victim's interests rather than 'views' in weighing up prosecution in the public interest. In notice of transfer cases, the Director of Public Prosecutions must certify that the case should proceed without delay at the Crown Court for the purpose of avoiding prejudice to the welfare of the child. This certification makes the provision of information about the child's interests particularly important. Only 18 post-Act CPS case files contained written information from the police indicating the wishes or interests of the child. There is no standard form for transmission of information to the CPS about the child's wishes and interests or other background material, though at least one CPS office has instituted a checklist for this purpose to be kept updated by the police.

CPS staff do not routinely meet witnesses and must rely on police opinions or on watching a videotaped interview in order to assess the impression child witnesses are likely to make and how well they may stand up to cross-examination. In October 1992 the police introduced the MG6, a standard Confidential Information Form which invites officers to comment on the 'strength and weakness or vulnerability of the witness'. Although information was provided in 77 of our 200 cases, it was mostly superficial.

Further information from the carer, police or social worker about the child's wishes and interests would assist the prosecutor in notice of transfer decisions, applications for TV link or screens and in deciding whether to accept a plea to a lesser charge, and would also act as a useful indicator of the need for additional pre-trial support for the child.

> An annex to the MG6 Confidential Information Form should be developed. This should distinguish the child's wishes and interests and cover the child's and carer's views about going to court, the manner in which the child would prefer to give evidence, therapy-related issues, whether there is a social services file about the child or family, and whether the child is the subject of parallel care proceedings.
>
> The police should routinely provide information on the MG6 under the heading 'strength and weakness or vulnerability of the witness'. This should be expanded to address the factors suggested by the Memorandum of Good Practice to be taken into consideration by those interviewing the child, for example the child's developmental stage, linguistic and emotional development and attention span (para. 2.3).

The 'List of Witnesses to Attend Court' allows the CPS to distinguish juvenile witnesses to the police. In our study, only 41 per cent of the children who were fully bound to attend court were identified as juveniles. 'Witness warning', the process by which witnesses are notified when to attend court, is usually carried out by police administrative units, not the investigative officers with whom the witnesses are already familiar and who are aware of cases requiring special sensitivity. Officers in CPUs generally wanted to be able to notify vulnerable witnesses personally about court attendance, but expressed concern that they were not always asked to do so because it was an exception to routine police procedures.

Juvenile witnesses should always be identified as such on witness lists. Witness warning procedures should take account of the need for vulnerable witnesses to be notified about court appearances by investigative officers.

A structure for inter-agency liaison

In 1990, the Working Group on Pre-Trial Issues reported that liaison meetings among criminal justice system agencies, usually hosted by the Crown Court, were essential in order to improve pre-trial performance (para. 349). Judges have a crucial role to play in overseeing policy implementation in this area, and reporting on a pilot project in 1994, the Group found that the direct involvement and guidance of the resident judge was a key factor (para. 125). The National Operational Practice Service Standard issued by the CPS in 1994 places equal emphasis on giving priority to child abuse cases and to liaison with other agencies so that issues of concern are addressed.

The Criminal Justice Consultative Council is an inter-disciplinary body, established as a result of Lord Justice Woolf's Inquiry into the 1990 Prison Disturbances which recommended the creation of an integrated liaison structure. After the close of fieldwork for this study, the Council agreed that child abuse cases should be put on a fast track (*The Times*, 26 October 1993). The singling out of a category of cases in this way was described as 'unprecedented'. The Council did not appear to be aware that priority for child abuse cases has been government policy since 1988. Lord Justice Farquharson, the Council chairman, circulated to 24 Area Committees details of a fast track scheme for child witness cases developed by Peterborough Crown Court. He suggested that the Area Committees should introduce similar procedures 'with such modifications as may be necessary for the courts concerned' (letter to the authors, 3 November 1993). There is no statutory or other formal sanction for failure to comply with the Peterborough scheme, 'but those who fall behind must be prepared to give a full explanation to the court'. The fast track scheme provides for a first appearance at court within three days of charge, and for transfer or committal to the Crown Court within 37 or 44 days respectively of the first magistrates' court appearance. However, the Peterborough schedule fails to set down target times for action at the Crown Court.

We contacted the Area Committees in March 1994 to enquire about progress. At that time, 14 out of 24 had discussed the Council's proposal. Some had set up sub-committees to consider the topic, but only two had implemented a fast tracking scheme. Although Committees lacked any local or national statistics with which to assess the extent of the problem, a minority conclusively decided not to adopt the Peterborough or similar scheme. Deliberations at five Committees were described to us as reflecting a degree of 'complacency and self-satisfaction' about the current situation, and one Committee suggested that imposition of a 'mechanistic' scheme to give priority to child abuse cases denigrated the professionals within the system. The Criminal Justice Consultative Council discussed the issue again in October 1994 but took no further action. It is waiting for feedback from those areas which have adopted fast track schemes.

Although the initial response of the Area Committees was disappointing, inter-agency liaison is being facilitated by other means. In Birmingham, the NSPCC has convened the Child Witness Consortium to which relevant groups are invited. In other areas, child witness issues have been taken forward under the auspices of the Area Child Protection Committee or Crown Court Users' Group. Some CPS offices have declined to participate in local committees; however, as a result of the CPS Service Standard described above which emphasises liaison with outside agencies, this attitude may be changing.

THE WAY FORWARD

Lord Justice Woolf's Inquiry into the 1990 Prison Disturbances found a 'geological fault' of inadequate communication and coordination across the agencies of the criminal justice system (para. 10.169). These failures are also evident in relation to the speedy progress policy. Cases in our study took much longer to dispose of than the national average, despite government policy and statute intended to give them priority. We have tried to describe ways in which greater coordination can be achieved and communication improved.

In the debate on the Criminal Justice Bill, the government rejected full implementation of the Pigot Report recommendations in the face of support by the Law Society, the Criminal Bar Association and the Council of Her Majesty's Circuit Judges (Spencer and Flin 1993, pp. 88–9). Lord Mackay of Clashfern, the Lord Chancellor, acknowledged that if, after the Act, 'delays were still endemic in the system', then the government would give further consideration to the full Pigot proposals (Hansard 139-140, 21 May 1991). Although our findings suggest that delay may indeed be endemic, we are not confident that implementation of the remaining Pigot recommendations (if introduced on a discretionary basis, like previous reforms) would adequately protect the interests of children. Three fundamental questions need to be addressed.

Has the introduction of technology masked the need for basic system and attitudinal changes?

The child witness reforms of the Criminal Justice Act 1991 gave equal emphasis to technological innovation (the admissibility of videotaped inter-views and extended eligibility for TV links) and the acknowledgement that pre-trial delay was prejudicial to children's interests. Millions of pounds have been spent on equipping video suites for use by the police and social workers, and on specialist training in the conduct of videotaped interviews. As of March 1994, link facilities have been installed in 53 Crown Court centres (some have more than one) at a cost of £30,000 per installation (letter from Lord Chancellor's Department, 18 February 1994). The commitment to assign child abuse cases to a fast track has been virtually ignored, while technological advances have been hailed by politicians as the primary solution to the trauma suffered by child witnesses. Projects undertaken on behalf of the US National Institute of Justice and the Australian Law Commission have warned that technology is not a panacea in resolving difficulties facing child witnesses (Whitcomb 1986, pp. 90–4; Cashmore and De Haas 1992, para. 7.87). A follow-up project in the US described videotaped interviews as a 'double-edged sword' (Whitcomb 1992, p. 150). The TV link and videotaped interview are highly visible and expensive 'solutions' which many experts agree have barely impinged on the underlying problem of secondary abuse of children by the criminal justice system (see, for example, Report of the Michael Sieff Foundation Annual Conference, September 1993).

The introduction of technology, if not based on a full understanding of the problems it is intended to solve, is not likely to produce the desired benefits. Despite the sizeable financial investment in the installation of equipment in courts, the study identified an undercurrent of resistance to TV link use on the part of some CPS staff, lawyers and judges. Screens were used more often than the link when children gave evidence at Crown Court in both pre- and post-Act trials.

What are the training needs of judges and lawyers?

The successful implementation of a fast track procedure for child abuse cases requires close inter-agency cooperation and active involvement by the judiciary. The failure thus far of the policy to expedite child abuse cases underlines the need for a case management training programme for all relevant personnel. (There are an increasing number of recommendations for improved case management of criminal cases, for example the recommendations of the Royal Commission on Criminal Justice, the Working Group on Pre-Trial Issues, and the Standing Commission on Efficiency.)

While reforms were intended to apply to a wide range of child victims and witnesses, the exercise of judicial discretion has operated to undermine the broad purpose of legislative intent because many judges have interpreted the new provisions rigidly and restrictively. The project came across a number of examples of what the Director of Public Prosecutions has condemned as 'justice by geography' (Victim Support Annual Conference, 8 November 1993). While there were local pockets of good practice, there were also courts where the legal culture inhibited the use of discretionary procedures on behalf of children. We were told of areas in which the videotaping of interviews with children had almost stopped because of the response of local judges. In a court outside our study, the CPS reported that the resident judge has instituted a policy concerning the use of videotaped evidence, in which tapes involving children under 10 will probably be accepted but 'he would need a great deal of convincing' to admit the tapes of children over 12. In one major court centre in our study, TV link equipment was used in only two out of 26 trials in which children gave evidence. Such policies ignore the intent of the legislation and fail to give any weight to the child's preference about how to give evidence. The Australian Law Reform Commission found that children's ability to choose whether or not to give evidence via TV link had a more significant effect on their emotional state, perceptions of the court experience and performance at court than the use of the link itself (Cashmore and De Haas 1992, para. 7.72). Training should address the making of informed decisions relating to the needs of individual children.

The Children Act Advisory Committee intends to explore the possibility of providing judges trained in the Children Act to hear child abuse cases in the Crown Court (*Second Annual Report* 1993, p. 16). Most judges do not have any professional background in dealing with children. We came across instances suggesting that training for judges, as for other professionals in the field, should address the effects of abuse. For example, in one study case a judge said of a six-year-old girl that a sexual assault 'would not have affected her'. In another, a judge said of a boy of six, whose case took 11 months to come to trial and who had been refused therapy while it was pending, 'he was none the worse for what happened'. In 1993, the Michael Sieff Foundation Annual Conference recommended that a new coordinated package be developed relating to children's welfare in criminal proceedings 'so that the judiciary can increase its awareness and understanding'.

Research has demonstrated that members of the legal profession need training in communicating with children in an age-appropriate manner (for example, Davies and Noon 1991, p. 139; Flin et al. 1993, pp. 319–39; Kranat and Westcott 1994, pp. 21–3). Judges also need greater awareness in order to recognise inappropriate questions and not compound the problem by asking confusing questions themselves. The *Child Witness Pack* advises children to tell the judge if they do not understand the questions, but responsibility should not fall wholly on the child. There is no equivalent advice for the judiciary or the Bar. During the cross-examination of an 11-year-old girl in one of our study cases, the judge made 32 interjections in the first 20 pages of her transcript testimony. Here is one example:

Defence counsel: 'Because I have to suggest to you, so that you understand, that you are not telling us the truth about that, do you see? That is the suggestion I make.'

Judge: 'Do you agree? Do you say that you are telling the truth, or do you say that you are not?'
Child: 'Yes.'

There is a school of thought which believes that defence counsel rarely intimidate or deliberately confuse child witnesses, because such behaviour might alienate the jury. The experience of this project suggests otherwise. We learned of instances in which the stress of testimony on the child brought on not only tears but vomiting, asthma attacks and, in one case, an epileptic seizure. (We found other examples of stress due to anticipation of going to court, including suicide attempts and prolonged absences from school.) The Pigot Report concluded that 'We cannot emphasise strongly enough that those children who are clearly upset or who break down in the witness-box simply manifest openly the effects of a much more generally harmful experience' (para. 2.12). The traumatic reality was sometimes acknowledged by lawyers on both sides. In a submission to the Crown Court relating to the taxation of costs, the defence barrister argued that his fee should be increased because the case 'required extensive preparation for a detailed and precise cross-examination of this young girl [aged 12], together with a full attack on her as to her previous sexual experience, her veracity and her character'. In another case, the CPS told the police to warn the child that 'she can expect the defence will give her no quarter'.

In the United States, the Department of Justice has urged judges to take a more active role in overseeing a child's participation at trial and to set ground rules for lawyers' behaviour before the child gives evidence (Whitcomb 1992, pp. 153–4). In the 1989 training video for judges and lawyers, 'When children are witnesses', written and produced by Doctors Laurie and Joseph Braga, Judge Judith C. Chirlin of the Los Angeles Superior Court demonstrates how the judge can ensure that the treatment of child witnesses is age-appropriate without prejudicing the rights of the defendant.

Despite case law indicating that judges in this country have the power to intervene in inappropriate cross-examination, they rarely do so (R v Wyatt [1990] CLR 343; R v Stretton (1988) 86 Cr App R 7). Different judges told us they feel that they cannot curtail cross-examination where the child clearly does not understand the questions, is intimidated by the barrister's face looming up close on the TV screen or is visibly distressed. Mr Justice Kay, who presided over the eight-month trial of a paedophile ring, has apparently told the Home Secretary he was 'powerless to stop a barrage of hostile questioning during the trial' (Daily Telegraph, 10 August 1994).

The Royal Commission recommended that judges take a more interventionist role and 'should be particularly vigilant to check unfair and intimidatory cross-examination by counsel of witnesses who in the nature of the case are likely to be distressed or vulnerable' (recommendation 201). This view has been endorsed by the Lord Chief Justice who said 'The role of the judge should not be restricted to that of an umpire sitting well above the play'. On the contrary, the interests of justice may require judicial intervention to protect witnesses (*Daily Telegraph*, 4 October 1994). Those involved with child witnesses should ask the judge before the trial starts to direct both counsel to use language appropriate to the developmental age of the child, and to arrange for breaks in testimony based on the child's attention span. Judges should reinforce the messages of the *Child Witness Pack* used in preparing children for court, by asking them to say if they do not understand a question, and by confirming that it is all right to reply that they 'don't know' or 'can't remember'.

At the time of writing, the issue of judicial training in relation to child witnesses is under active consideration by the Judicial Studies Board.

Can the status of the child be improved?

Children, like adults, have no choice in law about going to court as witnesses. This places a heavy onus on the criminal justice system to safeguard their interests. The Pigot Report, in advocating procedures which would transfer the taking of children's evidence from the trial to the pre-trial stage, wanted:

> [A] guarantee that children should not be required to give evidence against their wishes . . . children . . . ought never to be required to appear in public as witnesses in the Crown Court, whether in open court or protected by screens or closed circuit television, *unless they wish to do so*. This principle . . . is not only absolutely necessary for their welfare, but is also essential in overcoming the reluctance of children and their parents to assist the authorities. (paras. 2.22, 7.14; emphasis added)

If discretionary measures were introduced to allow videotaped cross-examination of the child witness at an out-of-court pre-trial hearing, it is probable that, like other procedures, they would not be used extensively. Moreover, such a reform would do nothing to bring children into the decision-making process. The implementation of the Pigot proposal giving children and their carers a choice about how and whether the child's evidence should be given at court would be of greater benefit to the child's welfare.

We believe there is a need to go beyond Pigot and consider the appointment of a specific individual with responsibility for the welfare of the child witness both before and at court, akin to the role of the guardian *ad litem* in care proceedings (Plotnikoff 1990; Morgan and Williams 1992). The Children Act Advisory Committee has expressed the intention to 'consider the position of the guardian *ad litem* where the child is a witness in criminal proceedings' (*Second Annual Report* 1993, p. 16). In the United States, there is a growing recognition that independent representation for the child may be just as critical in criminal as in civil cases (Whitcomb 1988, 1992). In this country, no one has specific responsibility for the welfare of the child witness in criminal proceedings. The *Child Witness Pack* advises that the person preparing the child for court 'will also be responsible for assessing a particular child's needs and passing this information to the police, CPS and court staff'. However, no resources have been allocated to child witness preparation, although research in North America suggests it may increase conviction rates and lower children's anxiety (Whitcomb 1992; London Family Court Clinic 1991). The Joint Letter from government departments which accompanied the *Child Witness Pack*, while listing the ideal criteria for the 'independent adult' to prepare the child for court, was conscious of the resource implications. It was careful to state only that 'there are many practitioners working in this field – both professional and voluntary – who could equally perform the role and it will be important to determine, in each individual case, who is best placed to do so'. Police officers, social workers and members of Victim Support and the Witness Service have told us there is much confusion about who is responsible for delivering the service.

In conclusion, we urge a fresh examination not only of measures related to the giving of evidence, but also of the need for system reforms – coordinated case management, priority listing, increased training for criminal justice system personnel and improved support for the child – which will benefit all children whose cases are prosecuted. The Michael Sieff Foundation Annual Conference in 1993 called for radical change because of 'the real concern that more children, families and professionals will opt out of the present process'. Despite the intention of legislative reforms, disillusionment with the system continues to grow.

REFERENCES

Bar Standards Review Body, (1994) *Blueprint for the Bar* (London: Bar Standards Review Body).

Cashmore, J. and De Haas, N. (1992), 'The use of closed-circuit television for child witnesses in the ACT', Research Paper 1 (Sydney: Australian Law Reform Commission).

Children Act Advisory Committee (1993), *Second Annual Report* (London: Lord Chancellor's Department).

Criminal Injuries Compensation Board (1992), *28th Annual Report* (London: HMSO).

Crown Prosecution Service (undated), *A Guide to Pre-Trial Issues within the Crown Prosecution Service* (London: Crown Prosecution Service).

Crown Prosecution Service (1993), *Statement on the Treatment of Victims and Witnesses by the Crown Prosecution Service* (London: Crown Prosecution Service).

Crown Prosecution Service (1994), *The Code for Crown Prosecutors* (London: Crown Prosecution Service).

Crown Prosecution Service (1994), *Explanatory Memorandum for use in connection with the Code for Crown Prosecutors* (London: Crown Prosecution Service).

Davies, G. and Noon, E. (1991), *An Evaluation of the Live Link for Child Witnesses* (London: Home Office).

Dent, H. and Flin, R. (eds.) (1992), *Children as Witnesses* (Chichester: John Wiley and Sons).

Department of Health and Social Security (1988), *Report of the Inquiry into Child Abuse in Cleveland 1987* (London: HMSO).

Flin, R., Bull, R., Boon, J. and Knox, A. (1993), 'Child Witnesses in Scottish Criminal Trials', *International Review of Victimology*, 2, pp. 319–39.

General Council of the Bar, *The Code of Conduct for the Bar of England and Wales* (fifth edition) (London: General Council of the Bar).

Gibbens, I. and Prince, J. (1963), *Child Victims of Sex Offences* (London: Institute for the Study and Treatment of Delinquency).

Glasgow, D., Horne, L., Calam, R. and Cox, A. (1994), 'Evidence, incidence, gender and age in sexual abuse of children perpetrated by children', *Child Abuse Review*, 3, pp. 196–210.

Goodman, G. and Bottoms, B. (1993), *Child Victims, Child Witnesses – Understanding and Improving Testimony* (New York: Guilford Press).

Graham Hall, J. and Martin, D. (1992), *Crimes Against Children* (Chichester: Barry Rose).

Home Office (1988), Circular 52/1988: The Investigation of Child Sexual Abuse.

Home Office (May 1988), Statistical Bulletin 42/89: Criminal Proceedings for Offences involving Violence against Children.

Home Office (1989), *Report of the Advisory Group on Video Evidence* (Chairman Judge Thomas Pigot QC) (London: Home Office).

Home Office (1990), *Victim's Charter. A Statement of the Rights of Victims of Crime* (London: Home Office).

Home Office (1991), White Paper, *Custody, Care and Justice: The Way Ahead for the Prison Service in England and Wales* (London: HMSO).

Home Office and Department of Health (1992), *Memorandum of Good Practice on Video Recorded Interviews with Child Witnesses for Criminal Proceedings* (London: HMSO).

Home Office, Department of Health, Department of Education and Science and the Welsh Office (1991), *Working Together under the Children Act 1989* (London: HMSO).

Kranat, V. and Westcott, H. (1994), 'Under fire: Lawyers questioning children in criminal courts', *Expert Evidence*, 3, pp. 16–24.

London Family Court Clinic (1991), *Reducing the system-induced trauma for child sexual abuse victims through court preparation, assessment and follow-up* (London, Ontario: The London Family Court Clinic).

Lord Chancellor's Department (1990), *Report of the Working Group on Pre-Trial Issues* (London: Lord Chancellor's Department).

Lord Chancellor's Department (1991), Judicial Statistics: Annual Report (London: Lord Chancellor's Department).

Lord Chancellor's Department (1992), Judicial Statistics: Annual Report (London: Lord Chancellor's Department).

Lord Chancellor's Department (1993, amended 1994), *Guidelines for Crown Court Listing* (London: Lord Chancellor's Department).

Lord Chancellor's Department (1994), *Pre-trial Issues Working Group Report – pilot study of Recommendation 92: Report of the National Steering Group* (London: Lord Chancellor's Department).

Morgan, J. and Plotnikoff, J. (1990), 'Children as victims of crime: procedure at court' in J. Spencer, G. Nicholson, R. Flin and R. Bull (eds.), *Children's Evidence in Legal Proceedings: an International Perspective* (Cambridge: Cambridge Law Faculty).

Morgan, J. and Williams, J. (1992), 'Child Witnesses and the Legal Process', *Journal of Social Welfare and Family Law*, 6, pp. 484–96.

Morgan, J. and Zedner, L. (1992), *Child Victims: Crime, Impact and Criminal Justice* (Oxford: Clarendon Press).

National Center for Prosecution of Child Abuse (1993), *Investigation and Prosecution of Child Abuse* (Alexandria, Va. USA: American Prosecutors Research Institute).

NSPCC and ChildLine (1993), *Child Witness Pack* (London: NSPCC).

Plotnikoff, J. (1990), 'Support and Preparation of the Child Witness: Whose Responsibility?', *Journal of Law and Practice*, 1, pp. 21–32.

Plotnikoff, J. and Woolfson, R. (1993), *From Committal to Trial: Delay at the Crown Court*, Standing Commission on Efficiency: Research Study No. 11 (London: The Law Society).

Reeves, P. (1991), 'The Cab Rank Rule', *Justice of the Peace*, pp. 780–81.

Rickford, F. (1992), 'Trials and Error', *Social Work Today*, 5 April 1992.

Royal Commission on Criminal Justice (1993), *Report* (Cm 2263) (London: HMSO).

Royal Commission on Criminal Justice (1993), *Crown Court Study: Research Study No. 19* (London: HMSO).

Sampson, A. (1994), *Acts of Abuse: Sex Offenders and the Criminal Justice System* (London: Routledge).

Scottish Law Commission (1990), *Report on the Evidence of Children and Other Potentially Vulnerable Witnesses* (SLC No. 125).

Seabrook, R. (1992), *The Efficient Disposal of Business in the Crown Court: Report of a Working Party* (London: The General Council of the Bar).

Sieff Foundation (1993), *Working Together for Children's Welfare: Child Protection and the Criminal Law*, Report of the Annual Conference (Virginia Water, Surrey: Michael Sieff Foundation).

Social Science Forum (September 1991), *Improving Government Statistics: Gaps and Discontinuities in Official Statistics*.

Spencer, J., Nicholson, G., Flin, R. and Bull, R. (1990), *Children's Evidence in Legal Proceedings: an International Perspective* (Cambridge: Cambridge University Law Faculty).

Spencer, J.R. and Flin, R. (1993), *The Evidence of Children: the Law and the Psychology* (2nd edn) (London: Blackstone Press).

Standing Commission on Efficiency (1990), *The Crown Court: A Guide to Good Practice for the Courts: The Lord Chancellor's Department* (London: HMSO).

Standing Commission on Efficiency (1990), *The Crown Court: A Guide to Good Practice for the Courts: The General Council of the Bar* (London: HMSO).

Standing Commission on Efficiency (1990), *The Crown Court: A Guide to Good Practice for the Courts: The Crown Prosecution Service* (London: HMSO).

United Nations (1991), *Convention on the Rights of the Child* (Cm 1668) (London: HMSO).

Walker Perry, N. and Wrightsman, L. (1991), *The Child Witness: Legal Issues and Dilemmas* (London: Sage Publications).

Wasik, M. and Taylor, R. (1991), *Blackstone's Guide to the Criminal Justice Act 1991* (London: Blackstone Press).

Wattam, C. (1993), *Making a Case in Child Protection* (London: NSPCC Longman).

Whitcomb, D.(1986), 'Child victims in court – the limits of innovation', *Judicature*, 70, pp. 90–4.

Whitcomb, D. (1988), *Guardians ad Litem in Criminal Courts* (Washington DC: National Institute of Justice).

Whitcomb, D. (1992), *When the Victim is a Child* (2nd edn) (Washington DC: National Institute of Justice).

Woolf, The Right Hon. Lord Justice and Tumin, His Honour Judge Stephen (1991), *Prison Disturbances April 1990 Report of an Inquiry* (Cm 1456) (London: HMSO).

Wright Dziech, B. and Schudson, C. (1991), *On Trial: America's Courts and Their Treatment of Sexually Abused Children.* (Boston: Beacon Press).

Zander, M. (November 1994), 'Report of the Bar Standards Review Body', *Legal Action*, 8.

INDEX

Crown Prosecution Service is used as a main heading, elsewhere **CPS** is used

Area Child Protection Committee 95
Australian Law Commission 96

Bail 38
Bar Guide to Good Practice 51
Bar Standards Review Body 51
Best interests of child *see* Interest of child

Care proceedings
    disclosure of records 63–4
    parallel prosecutions 62–3
Case management
    accountability 87
    clear definitions 82–3
    CPS responsibility 90–1
    informed decision-making concerning
        child's welfare 92–4
    inter-agency liaison 94–5
    performance monitoring 85–7
    policy guidance 83–4
    pre-trial process 87–90
    see also Identification of cases
Case Preparation Package (Crown Court)
    4, 51, 90–1
Charge decision 37–8
Child abuse
    definition 4, 7–8, 11, 44
    identification of cases *see* Identification of
        cases
Child abuse cases, requirement for records
    3
Child liaison officers (Crown Court) 15,
    72, 74–5, 87
Child neglect 34
Child prostitution 35
Child protection case conference 54
Child protection units (police) 34–5
    prosecution decision 53–4

Child Witness Consortium 95
Child Witness Form 9
Child witnesses 3–4
    age of child 39–40
    assessment of ability 39–40
    bystander witnesses 17
    Child Witness Pack 52
    committal proceedings 68
    cross-examination 7, 39, 98
    expedition of cases 4
    giving evidence against their wishes 99
    independent adult 52
    influence of delay 5–6
    police informing CPS of ability 39–40
    screens 49, 67, 75–8
    training required for treatment of 96–9
    TV links *see* TV links
    video-recorded interviews *see* Videotaped
        interviews
    warning 41–2
    witness orders 40–1
Children Act Advisory Committee 97
Children's Evidence Form 9
Civil care proceedings *see* Care proceedings
Code of Conduct for the Bar 51
Code for Crown Prosecutors, The 54, 55
Committal proceedings
    old style 67–8
    'paper' 67
Confidential Information Form MG6 39,
    93
Court Service Agency 1
Courts 65–81
    responsibility to give priority 66
    see also Crown Court: Magistrates' courts
CREST computerised listing system 69
Criminal Injuries Compensation Board 7
Criminal Justice Consultative
    Council 94–5
'Criming' 33–4
Cross-examination 7, 9

Cross-examination – *continued*
  inappropriate 98
Crown Court
  allocation of cases 69–71, 90
  case preparation 45
  child liaison officers 15, 72, 74–5, 87
  CREST computerised listing system 69
  delaying factors 70–1
  Guidelines for Crown Court Listing 71, 72,
    87, 88, 89
  identification of cases 68–9
  listing cases 71–3
    CREST system 69
    directions hearings 73, 83–9
    'fixed date' 72–3, 87
    'floaters' 71
    pre-trial review 73
    priority listing requests 49–50, 87
    'warned list' 71
  outcome of project cases 22–3
  screens 75–8
  time to disposition of project cases 26–8
    defendant's plea and 28
    Working Group on Pre-Trial Issues
      recommendations 30–1
  TV links 69, 75–8, 91–2
  videotaped interviews 79–81
Crown Court Case Preparation Package 4,
  51, 90–1
Crown Court Users' Group 95
Crown Prosecution Service 1
  application for use of screen or TV
    link 49
  child abuse case records requirement 3
  Crown Court case preparation 45
  definition of child abuse 4
  expedited hearing request 49–50, 87
  giving priority to child abuse 44
  *Guide to Pre-Trial Issues within the Crown
    Prosecution Service* 42
  identification of cases 44–5
    files from police 39–40
  interest of child and
    communication of wishes by police
      57–9
    prosecution decision 54–5
  List of Witnesses to Attend Court
    (LWAC form) 41, 42, 93
  magistrates' courts cases preparation 45
  Memorandum of Good Practice 55, 57–9,
    90
    interest of child 92–4
    pre-trial therapy 61
    transcripts of videotaped interviews 79
  monitoring progress of cases 45–6, 48
  National Field Inspectorate 43

Crown Prosecution Service – *continued*
  National Operational Practice Service
    Standard 1, 43, 44, 45, 46, 50, 83,
    85–6
  notice of transfer
    eligibility 46–7
    experience of 48–9
    monitoring cases 48
    right to appeal 47
    timing of decision to issue notice 47
  police and
    identification of files referred 38–9
    informing of child's ability as witness
      39–40
    pre-charge advice 36
  Policy Group 43
  pre-charge advice to police 36
  prosecution decision 54–5
  prosecutors 45–6
  responsibility for case management 90–1
  return of brief by prosecution counsel
    50–1
  SCOPE 45

Decision to prosecute *see* Prosecution
  decision
Defendant 19–20
  plea 28
  relationship with child 20
Delay
  Crown Court 70–1
  influence on children 5–6
  speedy progress requirement 6
  see also Speedy progress policy; Time to
    disposition of project cases
Departmental Committee on Sexual
  Offences against Young Persons 9
Directions hearing 73, 88–9
Disclosure of information
  care proceedings 63–4
  interest of child and 56
  pre-trial therapy 62

Expedited hearing request 49–50, 87

Forms
  Confidential Information Form MG6
    39, 93
  List of Witnesses to Attend Court
    (LWAC form) 41, 42, 93

*Guide to Pre-Trial Issues within the Crown
  Prosecution Service* 42
Guidelines for Crown Court Listing 71, 72,
  87, 88, 89

Identification of cases
  CPS 44–5
  Crown Court 68–9
  files referred from police to CPS 39–40
  flagging 38–9, 84–5
  logged cases 44–5
  magistrates' courts 66–7
  monitoring progress 45–6
  project cases 13–14
  systematic 84–5
  Working Group on Pre-Trial Issues
    recommendations 39
'Independent adult' 52
Inter-agency practice
  absence of 11
  liaison 94–5
Interest of child 4
  communication of wishes 57–9
  Confidential Information Form MG6
    39, 93
  decision making and 56–7, 92–4
  disclosure of information 56
  'independent adult' 52
  informed decision–making 92–4
  notice of transfer certification 53
  pre-trial therapy 4, 56, 59–62
  prosecution decision 53–5
  social services liaison 62–4
  taking into account 52–64
*Investigation and Prosecution of Child
  Abuse* 84

Judges
  allocation of cases to 69–71, 87–8
  continuity of involvement 87–8
  discretion
    use of TV links or screens 75–6, 78
    use of videotaped interviews 96–7
  interventionist role 98–9
  training for child cases 96–9

Lawyers, training for child cases 96–9
List of Witnesses to Attend Court
  (LWAC form) 41, 42, 93
Listing cases *see* Crown Court, listing cases

Magistrates' courts
  case preparation 45
  identification of cases 66–7
  management of child abuse cases 66–7
  old-style committals 67–8
  outcome of project cases 21
  paper committals 67
  screens for child witnesses 67
  time to disposition of project cases 26,
    29–30

Magistrates' courts – *continued*
  Working Group on Pre-Trial Issues
    recommendations 29–3
  transfer procedure 68
Management of cases *see* Case management
Medical examinations 18–19
Memorandum of Good Practice 55, 57–9, 90
  interest of child 92–4
  pre-trial therapy 61
  transcripts of videotaped interviews 79
Michael Sieff Foundation Annual
  Conference (1993) 96, 97, 100

National Association for the Welfare of
  Children in Hospital 1
National Centre for the Prosecution of Child
  Abuse (US) 84
National Institute of Justice (US) 96
National Operational Practice Service
  Standard 1, 43, 44, 45, 46, 50, 83
  monitoring performance 85–6
Notice of transfer 4, 25, 27, 92
  certification that case will proceed
    without delay 53
  eligibility for 46–7
  experience of 48–9
  monitoring cases 48
  right to appeal 47
  timing of decision to issue notice 47
NSPCC 95

Offences 20–1

Patten, John 6
Performance monitoring 85–7
Pigot Report 6, 99
  requirement for statistics 8
  video-recorded interviews 6–7
Police
  bail 38
  child protection units 34–5, 53–4
  Confidential Information Form MG6
    39, 93
  CPS and
    identification of files referred 38–9
    informing of child's ability as witness
      39–40
    pre-charge advice 36
  identification of files 39–40
  interest of child and
    communication of wishes to CPS
      57–9
    prosecution decision 53–4
  interviews
    jointly with social workers 36
    videotaped 35

Police – *continued*
  investigation of offences against children
    34–6
    child protection units 34–5, 53–4
    conventional methods 35–6
    pre-charge advice from CPS 36
    prosecution decision 37–8, 53–4
    recording the crime 33–4
    reporting of offence 32–3
    videotaped interview training 35
Pre-trial process 87–90
Pre-trial review 73
Pre-trial therapy *see* Therapy
Project cases
  child profiles 16–18
    ages 17
    numbers per case 16–17
  data
    collection 14–15
    quality 14
  defendants 19–20
  distribution 16
  identification of 13–14
  interviews 15
  medical examinations 18–19
  offences
    class 20
    nature of 21
    number of counts 20
  outcome
    Crown Court 22–3
    magistrates' courts 21
  selection criteria 11–13
  sentences 23–4
Prosecution decision 37–8
  CPS 54–5
  interest of child 53–5
  police child protection units 53–4
Prosecutors 45–6
  return of brief 50–1

Recording the crime 33–4
*Report of the Advisory Group on Video
  Evidence* 6
*Report of the Inquiry into Child Abuse in
  Cleveland 1987* 34
Reporting of offence 32–3
  time between offence and report 33

SCOPE 45
Screens
  application for use 49
  Crown Court 75–8
  magistrates' courts 67
Sentences, project cases 23–4
Social services
  disclosure of information 63–4

Social services – *continued*
  joint interviews with police 36
  parallel prosecution and care proceedings
    62–3
Speedy progress policy
  cases to which applies 7–8
  John Patten on 6
  lack of statistics 8–9
  need for evaluation 9–10
  see also Time to disposition of project cases
Summons decision 37–8

Therapy
  dangers of pre-trial therapy 60
  decision about pre-trial therapy 56
  disclosure to defence 62
  interest of child 59–62
  prevention before trial 4
  tainting evidence 4
  videotaped interviews 60, 61–2
Time to disposition of project cases 25–31
  Crown Court 26–8
  magistrates' court 26, 29–30
  notice of transfer 25, 27
TV links 95–6
  application for use 49, 69, 91–2
  Crown Court 69, 75–8, 91–2
  evaluation 76–7
  reduction in impact of evidence 77–8

United Nations Convention on the Rights of
  the Child 55

Victim's Charter 6, 65, 85
  tagging files 38
Videotaped interviews 39, 60, 61–2, 95–6
  ages of children 17–18
  Crown Court use 79–81
  deferring decision about use 80–1
  geographical differences 96–7
  Pigot Report 6–7
  refreshing memory from 80
  technical and evidential quality 79–80
  training in conduct of 35
  transcripts 79

'Warned list' 71
Warning of witnesses 41–2
Witness orders 40–1
  see also Child witnesses
Witnesses
  List of Witnesses to Attend Court 41,
    42, 93
  'up to proof' 67
Working Group on Pre-Trial Issues 1, 71,
    72, 85–7
  continuity of judge's involvement 88

Working Group on Pre-Trial Issues –
 continued
 either way offences
   committed or transferred for trial   30
   tried summarily   29
 identification of files   39
 recommendations   28–30
   Crown Court   31

Working Group on Pre-Trial Issues –
 continued
   magistrates' court   29–3
   witness orders   41
 *Working Together under the Children Act
   1989*   4, 44, 83
 pre-trial therapy   60–1
 prosecution decision   53–4